Corporate Information Factory

W.H. Inmon

Claudia Imhoff

Ryan Sousa

WILEY COMPUTER PUBLISHING

New York • Chichester • Weinheim • Brisbane • Singapore • Toronto

This book would not have been possible without the unflagging support of our families. They remain the wind beneath our wings and the joy in our hearts.

—C., R., & B.

Publisher: Robert Ipsen
Editor: Robert Elliott
Assistant Editor: Pam Sobotka
Managing Editor: Micheline Frederick
Text Design & Composition: Publishers' Design and Production Services, Inc.

This text is printed on acid-free paper.

Library of Congress Cataloging-in-Publication Data:

Inmon, William H.
    Corporate information factory/W.H. Inmon, Claudia Imhoff, Ryan Sousa.
        p.   cm.
    "Wiley computer publishing."
    Includes bibliographical references and index.
    ISBN 0-471-19733-5 (cloth : alk. paper)
    1. Information storage and retrieval systems—Business.   2. Business—Data processing.   3. Database management.   4. Data warehousing.   I. Imnoff, Claudia. II. Sousa, Ryan, 1964– .   III. Title.
    HF5548.2.I4264 1998
    658.4′038—dc21   97-29023
                                                                                                      CIP

Printed in the United States of America

10 9 8 7 6 5 4 3 2 1

Contents

Where We Came From

ome books describe *how* to do things—they're called how-to books or manuals. Other books describe *why* we do things; these include books on philosophy and psychology. Still other books describe *where* things are—for example, atlases. But other books simply describe *what* we should be doing. This is one of those kinds of books.

The usefulness of a *what* book is that it provides direction. (There is an old saying among sailors, "When there is no destination, any route will do.") This book describes a very substantial destination port for the sailors of the sea of information. Once the organization understands that there is a port and where it is, it is easy to set the information organization's rudder on the right heading to the appropriate destination, even through stormy seas.

THE ORIGINS OF DATA WAREHOUSING

The world of computers and information technology has grown quickly, sequentially, and in a surprisingly uniform manner. In the era of punch-card and paper-tape systems, we used the computer as a calculating beast of burden, running such systems as accounts payable and accounts receivable.

With the advent of disk storage, cheaper memory, more sophisticated operating systems, and direct end-user interface devices, a whole new style of computing became a reality—online processing. With online processing the computer changed from a beast of burden to an Arabian stallion. Reservation systems, automated bank tellers, and a host of other new systems became a reality.

Next came the revolution of the end user. Personal computers, spreadsheet applications, and fourth-generation language (4GL) technology opened up computing to an audience that previously had been denied. As the costs of computing plummeted, a Pandora's box was opened—computing now fell outside the classical domain of the information systems organization. Anyone with a budget could begin to take charge of his or her information destiny.

End users were very happy having such complete control, but this autonomy was a mirage. It soon became apparent that even with unlimited computing power, turning over control to end users created new issues, such as lack of integration and proper economies of scale. For all of the appeal of autonomous control of processing at the end-user level, the case for centralization was equally valid and appealing.

Simultaneously, people discovered that data derived from processing operational transactions was insufficient for effective decision-making. Historical and integrated data was needed at both a summary and detailed level.

Thus, the data warehouse was born. Shortly thereafter, data volumes and end-user demands and diversity exceeded the pace at which the data warehouse could be tailored and tuned. For all its strength in integrating and managing a common view of corporate data, the data warehouse was not keeping up with the business demands for information. In response, different departments found that a customized subset of the data warehouse—something called a data mart—provided them the needed autonomy to drive the interpretation and use of corporate information.

Some organizations also discovered that there was a need for operational integration at a collective level. The data warehouse—for all it provided—did nothing for the people who needed operational integration. Into the fray came an architectural entity known as the operational data store. Finally, data and processors were being glued together by a new generation of networks called intranets and a new generation of scalable, low cost computer systems classified as high-performance computing.

SEEING THE FOREST FOR THE TREES

Those of us who have been witnesses to some or all of these developments have suffered from two disadvantages in understanding what has transpired. First, we have been too close to the technology and the maturation of the technology to truly grasp its significance. We have marveled at the details without understanding the larger form and structure. As such, we, like the six blind men describing the elephant, simply have a limited understanding of that with which we are the most intimate.

The second disadvantage is that of watching this development unfold sequentially day by day. The speed of day-by-day developments has blinded us to the larger picture that is unfolding—and we can only guess what tomorrow will bring. This book attempts to overcome these obstacles in examining the evolving architecture of the corporate information ecosystem. The authors hope to make sense of the many advances that have been made in computing technology and show they affect the way business systems are built. The emphasis is on identifying the architectural components and showing how they fit together.

The authors are particularly interested in what happens when an organization attempts to build its systems in a fashion other than what has been suggested by the architecture. The architecture described in this book is hardly the only possibility for an information systems architecture. In many cases, it will be tempting to violate the architecture; however, systems designers must be aware that there is a price to pay when they do so.

Our purpose in writing this book is to alert readers that there is a proven way to organize information systems; that when this way is not chosen, they must be willing—and able—to live with the consequences. These consequences can range from the waste of large amounts of development resources to failure to deliver an effective information resource.

A number of factors led to the evolution of the corporate information factory (CIF) including:

- ❏ Evolving business demands
- ❏ Shrinking costs of technology
- ❏ Growth of hardware and software capabilities
- ❏ The birth of a whole new audience made up of not only technical people but accountants, marketers, sales people, and others.

In addition, corporate communities began to move toward very distinct styles of computing. For example, operational, legacy processing set the stage for the data warehouse, which then led to the data mart. Spreadsheets and their many derivatives opened up the desktop to many more analytical capabilities. These various benchmarks led to the evolution of a new mode of corporate computing which we describe in the chapters to follow.

WHO SHOULD READ THIS BOOK

The corporate information factory can be used in many useful ways by a wide variety of people, such as:

- ❏ **The IT manager.** The information technology (IT) manager can use the corporate information factory to predict what the next steps ought to be for systems development and architecture. Instead of spending money unproductively on projects that do not move the organization to the paradigm suggested by the corporate information factory, the manager who understands its implications can use the corporate information factory as a benchmark which tells what the future directions ought to be.

❏ **The developer.** Once a project has begun, the developer can determine whether the project is organized in concert with the corporate information factory. If a design is contrary to the corporate information factory, the designer can make corrections before the design is cast in concrete.

❏ **Investors.** An easy way to determine how fruitful a technology investment will be is to gauge it against the world described by the corporate information factory. If the architecture of the investment is not aligned with the corporate information factory, then the investor can be alerted to problems with marketplace acceptance.

❏ **The end user.** At the heart of the corporate information factory is the success of end users who can use it to form their expectations and assess whether their expectations are out of line. When implemented properly, the corporate information factory makes life very easy and productive for the end user.

HOW THIS BOOK IS ORGANIZED

The major architectural entities that make up the corporate information factory include:

❏ Operational, transaction-oriented systems (Application Environment)
❏ A data warehouse
❏ Data marts
❏ Networks (Internet and intranet)
❏ An operational data store (ODS)
❏ An integration and transformation (I & T) layer

There are many other components to the corporate information factory that will be discussed in this book as well, such as:

❏ Metadata
❏ Data models
❏ Reference data
❏ External data

❏ Unstructured data

❏ Archival data and processing, and more

THE EVOLUTION OF THIS BOOK

This book is part of a larger series of books by Bill Inmon. In the first of the books, *Data Architecture: The Information Paradigm*, the notion of a larger architecture was first introduced and the data warehouse was first mentioned. The next book in the series, *Building the Data Warehouse*, fully explored the data warehouse. The book is now enjoying sales in the second edition. Next came *Using the Data Warehouse*, in which the techniques and considerations of the effective use of the data warehouse were discussed and the operational data store was introduced. At about the same time, *Building the Operational Data Store* appeared. This book probed the design and technological implications of the ODS. The next book in the series was *Managing the Data Warehouse*. In this book, the assumption is that the data warehouse has already been built and that the issues of cost of data warehousing and complexity of data warehousing are starting to crop up.

The current book , *Corporate Information Factory*, in many ways is a capstone book. It brings together the many aspects of the architected information systems environment—the *information ecosystem*—and presents those aspects in an integrated manner.

Acknowledgments

The authors wish to express thanks to the many personal and professional colleagues who have contributed to this understanding of the information ecosystem.

Special thanks to:

John Zachman, Zachman International

David Imhoff, Intelligent Solutions

Jon Geiger, Intelligent Solutions

Lowell Fryman, Intelligent Solutions

Bob Conway, Intelligent Solutions

Joyce Norris-Montanari, Intelligent Solutions

Rob Geller, MCI Communications

Robert Grim, MCI Communications

Larry Greenfield, MCI Communications

warehouseMCI Team, MCI Communications

Dennis McCann, Pine Cone Systems

Debra Colombana, Pine Cone Systems

Ken Richardson, Pine Cone Systems

Bill Pomeroy, Pine Cone Systems

Philip Glynn, Pine Cone Systems

Roger Geiwitz, Pine Cone Systems

Dale Brocklehurst, Pine Cone Systems

Pete Simcox, Informix

Steve Hill, Informix

JD Welch, Data Wing Consulting

Kevin Gould, Sybase

Stephen Gardner, NCR

Jeanne Friedman, Logica

Greg Battas, Tandem Computers

Arnie Barnett, Barnett Data Systems

Ralph Kimball, Kimball and Associates

Marc Demarest, Sequent Computer Systems

CHAPTER ONE

Creating an Information Ecosystem

Business is quickly reshaping itself to compete in a global economy governed by the needs of the customer (e.g., individual, business, etc.). The economies gained over the past three decades by automating manual business processes are no longer enough to gain a competitive advantage in today's marketplace. To compete, businesses need to be able to build a new set of capabilities that deliver *best-of-breed* business intelligence and business management solutions that can leverage this legacy environment.

But wait! Perhaps the genesis is already upon us. Your IT department is being bombarded with a growing number of targeted information architectures, technologies, methodologies, terms, and acronyms. Each of these advances promises to deliver competitiveness in one easy step, such as:

❑ Data warehousing
❑ Data repository
❑ Operational data store

1

- ❏ Data marts
- ❏ Data mining
- ❏ Super store
- ❏ Internet and intranet
- ❏ Multidimensional and relational databases
- ❏ Star schema, snowflake, and relational database design techniques
- ❏ High-performance computing (Massively Parallel Processing & Symmetrical Multi-processing)
- ❏ Data acquisition, and data delivery
- ❏ Online Analytical Processing (OLAP)
- ❏ Data warehouse administration
- ❏ Metadata management

Each of these advances in modern information technology has promise, but trying to make sense of these point solutions while still getting the job done in a short time frame can be confusing and intimidating. This is largely due to the fact that no model exists that combines these elements of the information primordial pool into a balanced ecosystem that aligns to the evolving needs of the business. An information ecosystem is needed to orchestrate the use of various information technologies and constructs, and to foster communication and cooperative exchange of work, data, process, and knowledge as part of a symbiotic relationship.

INFORMATION ECOSYSTEM BRIEFLY DEFINED

An information ecosystem is a system with different components, each serving a community directly while working in concert with other components to produce a cohesive, balanced information environment. Like nature's ecosystem, an information ecosystem must be adaptable, changing as the inhabitants and participants within its aegis change.

Over time, the balance between different components and their relationship to each other changes as well, as the environment changes. Sometimes the effect will appear on seemingly unrelated parts (sometimes disastrously!). Adaptability, change, and balance are the hallmarks of the components of a healthy information ecosystem.

As an example of an information ecosystem, consider a data warehouse working with a data mart to deliver business intelligence capabilities or an operational data store working to deliver business management capabilities. This is exemplified by many marketing groups. At first, there is the need for better business intelligence in the form of market segmentation, customer profiling, customer profitability, and customer contact analysis. Then, at some point, marketing wants to take action on the "intelligence" gained. Though the data warehouse and data mart were well suited to support business intelligence, they lack the content and form to drive business management activities associated with contacting the customer. What is needed is an operational data store to provide near *real-time* access to integrated, current customer information.

As will be discussed in this book, different business needs require that a different set of ecosystem components work in tandem. Ultimately, the information ecosystem will be business-driven, as capabilities delivered (business intelligence and business management) are aligned to the needs of the business (marketing, customer care, product management, etc.). The result is an information environment that allows companies to capitalize on a constantly changing business landscape characterized by customer relationships and customized product delivery.

THE SHIFTING BUSINESS LANDSCAPE

Three fundamental business pressures are fueling the evolution of the information ecosystem: growing consumer de-

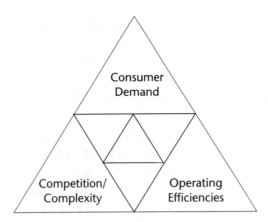

FIGURE 1.1
*The business drivers in
today's world.*

mand, increased competition and complexity, and continued demands for improvements in operating efficiencies as
seen in Figure 1.1.

The first fundamental pressure is growing consumer
demand. Consumers expect companies to understand and
respect their needs and desires. Since the customer drives
the business relationship, business people must hear what
the customer has to say, and respond by delivering relevant,
competitive, timely products and services. Companies can
no longer expect to sell just a few general products and
services to the masses, but must tailor many products and
services (i.e., mass customize) to the individual consumer.
This proposition is called relationship marketing and/or
mass customization. The fundamental challenge to many
businesses is that their systems, people, and processes are
aligned around the product. Furthermore, most of these
companies have begun to extend these environments with a
series of unarchitected point solutions to address their immediate needs for customer management. A healthy information ecosystem will be embodied by an architecture that:

❑ Leverages this legacy environment
❑ Delivers new information capabilities that allow
   companies to thrive in an environment characterized

by customer relationships and customized product delivery

❑ Supports a migration strategy that is evolutionary in nature and delivers incremental value to the business

The second business pressure is that of increased competition and complexity. The ability to refocus and enhance a product mix in response to evolving competition is a critical success factor for any business. The key is to be able to anticipate the needs of the marketplace before your competitors do. Many companies find this difficult or impossible to do, given today's mishmash of technologies, architectures, and systems.

Why is this important? Corporations today are facing more and more deregulation, mergers, and acquisitions which blur the relationships with their customers. Additionally, globalization of the marketplace and the consumer is opening up businesses to new avenues for expansion and subsequently, competition. Therefore, it is mandatory for a corporation to quickly restructure itself without losing the ability to compete.

The third pressure is that of continued improvements in operating efficiencies. The ability to rapidly measure and predict returns on investment is something that corporations find difficult to perform. These measurements indicate the health of the corporation and the ability to determine them rapidly allows a corporation to change its direction with a minimal loss in time or money. Other examples of improved efficiency include the ability to determine the most efficient channels for contacting customers, target the best product mix to the best customers, and the ability to identify new product opportunities before the competition does.

Responding to Change

In response to these very real business challenges, companies must be able to support more than just classical busi-

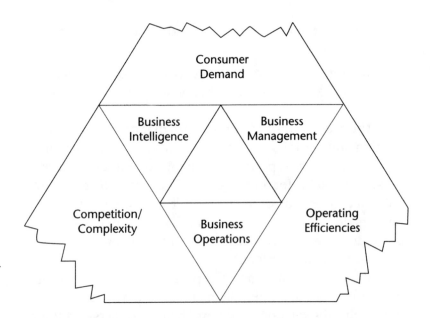

FIGURE 1.2

The need for business capabilities to compete in a quickly changing business landscape.

ness operations (legacy systems that automate manual business processes such as billing, order processing, etc.). Competitive corporations need capabilities to support business intelligence and business management. In this way, they can respond to the dynamics of a quickly changing business landscape, as seen in Figure 1.2.

The information ecosystem provides a context for understanding the needs of your business and taking actions based on those needs while still running the day-to-day business. Additionally, the information ecosystem provides businesses with a comprehensive model for leveraging the growing number of distinctive information constructs and technologies that are required to deliver diverse and pressing business capabilities to support these needs. Figure 1.3 illustrates the central role of the corporate information factory in supporting the evolving areas of business proficiency: business operations, business intelligence, and business management.

Business operations is supported by capabilities used to run the day-to-day business. These systems have tradi-

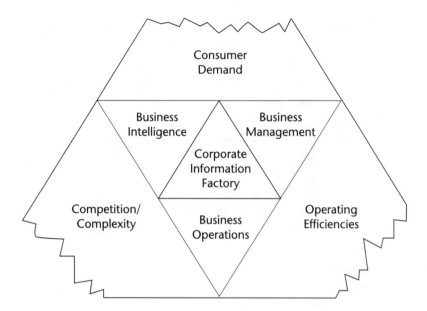

FIGURE 1.3

The corporate information factory is central to a business and its needed capabilities.

tionally made up our legacy environment and have provided a competitive advantage by automating manual business processes to gain economies of scale and speed-to-market. Systems that exemplify business operations include accounts payable, accounts receivable, billing, order processing, compensation, and lead list generation.

Business intelligence is supported by capabilities that help companies understand what makes the wheels of the corporation turn and help predict the future impact on current decisions. These systems play a key role in the strategic planning process of the corporation. Systems that exemplify business intelligence include medical research, customer profiling, market basket analysis, customer contact analysis, market segmentation, customer profiling, scoring, profitability trending, and inventory forecasting.

Business management is supported by capabilities that are needed to effectively manage actions resulting from the business intelligence gained. If business intelligence helps companies understand *what* makes the wheels of the corporation turn, business management helps *direct* the wheels as the business landscape changes. Systems that ex-emplify business management include product manage-ment, contact management, inventory management, resource management, and customer information manage-ment. These systems generally augment and/or evolve from business operations.

In summary, the information ecosystem provides com-panies with a complete information solution by complementing traditional business operations with capa-bilities to deliver business intelligence and business man-agement. In addition, the information ecosystem provides a comprehensive model for making sense and exploiting the growing and diverse information constructs and technolo-gies that are transforming our information paradigm. The physical embodiment of the information ecosystem is the corporate information factory.

THE CORPORATE INFORMATION FACTORY

First introduced by W. H. Inmon in the early 1980s, the cor-porate information factory (CIF) is the physical embodiment of the notion of an information ecosystem. The CIF is at the same time generic in its structure (to the point that it is eas-ily recognizable across different corporations) and is unique to each company and organization as it is shaped by cul-ture, politics, economics, and technology.

The corporate information factory is made up of the following components:

❑ **Applications.** The family of systems from which the corporate information factory gathers raw detailed data. There are two types of applications; integrated and unintegrated. Integrated applications represent those systems that have been developed according to the guidelines set forth by the corporate information factory. Unintegrated applications are traditionally represented by those core operational systems that

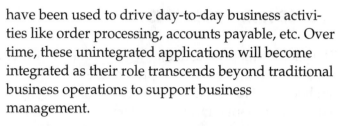

have been used to drive day-to-day business activities like order processing, accounts payable, etc. Over time, these unintegrated applications will become integrated as their role transcends beyond traditional business operations to support business management.

❏ **An integration and transformation layer.** Where the data gathered by the applications is refined into a corporate structure.

❏ **Data warehouse.** A subject-oriented, integrated, time-variant (temporal), and non-volatile collection of summary and detailed data used to support the strategic decision-making process for the enterprise.

❏ **Data mart.** Customized, summarized data from the data warehouse tailored to support the specific analytical requirements of a given business unit.

❏ **Operational data store.** A subject-oriented, integrated, current-valued, volatile collection of detailed data used to support the up-to-the-second collective tactical decision-making process for the enterprise.

❏ **Metadata.** The information catalog infrastructure to the corporate information factory. This catalog provides the necessary details to promote data legibility, use, and administration.

❏ **The Internet and Intranet.** The lines of communication along which data flows and different components interact with each other.

The different components of the CIF create a foundation for information delivery and decision-making activities that can occur anywhere in the CIF. Many of these activities are in the form of decision-support systems (DSS) that provide the end user with easy-to-use, intuitively simple tools to distill information from data.

PEOPLE AND PROCESSES

The people and processes that work within the structure of the information ecosystem represent the roles, workflow, methods, and tools used in constructing, managing and using the corporate information factory. Activities that occur here include:

- ❑ Customer communications (newsletters, surveys, etc.)
- ❑ Request management (logging, prioritizing, and managing)
- ❑ Delivery of information (data mart enhancements, corrections)
- ❑ Configuration management (versioning of metadata, database design, extraction and transformation programs, etc.)
- ❑ Data quality management (performing audits, integrity checks, alerts)
- ❑ Systems administration (determining capacity, conducting performance tuning, etc.)

The people and process of the CIF is perhaps one of the more difficult aspects for a corporation because, in planning this function, the corporation must take into consideration its culture, politics, economics, geography, change, and other concerns. For example, companies that have traditionally managed their information systems from a central organization may have challenges supporting data marts that are owned and managed by line-of-business information systems personnel. Alternatively, organizations that have managed information systems at the line-of-business level, may have problems giving up the control necessary to form an information systems group to build and manage a corporate data warehouse.

The nature of these variables makes this function a much more customized one for the enterprise and, therefore, harder to implement. There is less uniformity across different corporations in how this aspect of the information ecosystem is implemented than perhaps anywhere else.

SUMMARY

The information ecosystem is a model that supports all of a corporation's information processing. The physical embodiment of the information ecosystem is the corporate information factory. The different components of the corporate information factory have been introduced and defined briefly to give the information systems (IS) architect an idea of how they fit into the overall architecture. Each component must be in balance with the others to avoid a malfunctioning environment, much like nature's ecosystem.

The forces of business coupled with the advances in technology and the symbiotic relationship of technology to the business process cause the world of technology to constantly evolve. In years past when technology was slow and expensive, there was no opportunity for the sophistication that is possible today. But with the decreasing cost of technology, the increasing speed, and new capacities, there are possibilities for the exploitation of technology in the business equation as never before. At the heart of the possibilities is an evolving architecture which has become increasingly apparent, the corporate information factory. It has evolved from many systems and technologies now found in the world of corporate information processing.

In the next chapter, we will take a closer look at the corporate information factory, its use, and its evolution.

CHAPTER TWO

Introducing the Corporate Information Factory

As discussed in Chapter 1, the corporate information factory (CIF) is an architecture for the information ecosystem, consisting of the following architectural components:

❑ An applications environment

❑ An integration and transformation layer (I & T layer)

❑ A data warehouse with current and historical detailed data

❑ A data mart(s)

❑ An operational data store (ODS)

❑ An Internet and intranet

❑ A metadata repository

The simplest way to understand the corporate information factory is in terms of the flow of data that moves in and information that flows out of the corporate information factory. Data enters the corporate information factory as detailed, raw data collected by the applications environment.

The raw detailed data is refined by the applications, then passes into a layer of programs that fundamentally integrate and transform functional data into corporate data. The data passes from the integration and transformation layer into the ODS and the data warehouse. The data warehouse can be fed data from either the ODS or the integration and transformation layer. After the data passes through the data warehouse, it goes into a data mart. Throughout the various architectural components of the corporate information factory, data is accessed, analyzed, and transformed into information for various purposes.

The architecture and the flow of data that have been described are very similar to that of an actual factory. Raw and assembly goods enter a factory and are immediately collected by inventory and store management processors. Once entered into the factory, assembly lines turn the raw goods into a product. Throughout the manufacturing process, different products are made. Some products are completed and finished products; others represent a partial assembly that can be further assembled into many finished products.

DATA IN THE CORPORATE INFORMATION FACTORY

Key components of the corporate information factory are shown in Figure 2.1. Let's begin with external data. External data enters the corporate information factory from the world outside of the corporation. It is not generated internally, nor is it captured and manipulated at a detailed level internally. Instead, external data represents events and objects outside of the corporation in which the corporation is interested. External data can be used throughout the corporate information factory—at the data mart, data warehouse, ODS, and/or application levels.

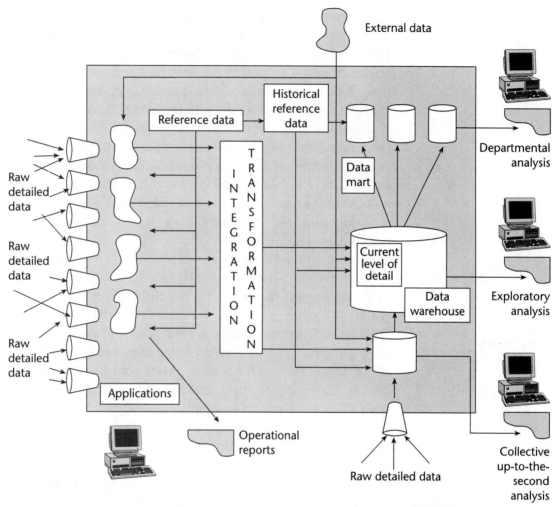

FIGURE 2.1
The basic structure of the corporate information factory.

Reference data is data that is stored in a short-hand fashion that serves to tie together multiple and diverse users. It is used to speed and standardize processing across many different departments and is typically found at the application level. As reference data passes into the architectural components of the corporate information factory, it takes on a slightly different form, that of historical reference data. The difference between reference data and historical reference data is that reference data represents information that is current and accurate as of the moment of usage. Historical reference data is the historical record of that same reference data, except that it is collected and managed over time. As current reference data changes over time, those changes are collected along with the effective date of the change in order to create historical reference data. Historical reference data is of great use to the data mart and the data warehouse analyst in that it provides details that help describe data in the data warehouse and data marts.

A third type of data is raw detailed data. This data is generally captured at the application level and loaded into the data warehouse and ODS via the I & T layer. However, some raw detailed data may be captured and managed directly in the ODS. This happens when the end-user community needs access to data that is not currently being managed by an application. In effect, the ODS becomes the authoritative source of this data and source system to the data warehouse. Some may try to manage this data directly in the data warehouse; however, this is not recommended. This would be like trying to bulldoze a large mound of dirt with a Ferrari. The data warehouse is designed for strategic decision support, and lacks the form and function to effectively administer transaction-level data. Additionally, if the data warehouse became the *authoritative* source of this raw detail data, it is likely that it would quickly become pressured to support operational activities for which it was designed to augment. This is likely to be a terminal condition for the information ecosystem.

Reference Data

Some of the most important data any corporation has is reference data. An example of a very popular type of reference data is data that describes valid products and product hierarchies for a company. Reference data fulfills the following roles:

❑ It allows a corporation to standardize on a commonly used name for important and frequently used information, such as product, states, countries, and so forth.

❑ It allows commonly used names to be stored and accessed in a short-hand fashion, which saves disk space.

❑ It provides the basis for consistent interpretation of corporate data across departments. For example, if reference data existed, we could be reasonably assured that three separate departments analyzing sales volumes for dog food would come up with the same answer. Without this reference data, each department is likely to roll-up products differently, resulting in different sales volumes for dog food.

In short, reference data is one of the most important kinds of data that a corporation has. Figure 2.2 shows the presence of reference data in the CIF.

Reference data is notoriously unstructured and is, at best, a hit and miss proposition. This is in contrast to other forms of data core to running the day-to-day business which requires and receives great care in systematization. For example, data is needed to invoice a customer correctly. Programs and procedures are written for the update, creation, and deletion of nonreference data. But because reference data is so commonly used, programs and procedures needed for the systematization of reference data are not formalized. There are several reasons for the lack of formalization:

❑ The volume of data that constitutes reference data is usually very small compared to other types of data found in the corporation. Reference data consumes only a fraction of a fraction of the space required for regular data. Because of its small size, reference data is often treated as an afterthought.

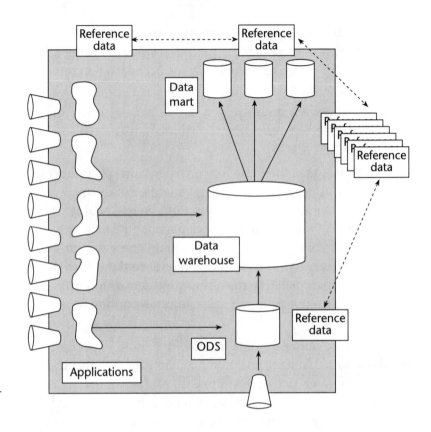

FIGURE 2.2

Reference data makes up an important part of the CIF. Note that reference data in the data warehouse is historical.

❏ Reference data is usually very slow to change. Unlike other types of data which are constantly being created, deleted, and updated, reference data is very stable. Because of this stability, no one pays attention to the need for systematization of reference data.

❏ Reference data is often dictated by external sources. There are standard abbreviations for states, countries, and so on. There is no need for systematization of these types of reference data.

❏ Reference data often belongs to the entire corporation, not just a single department. Because reference data is a common corporate property, no one steps forward to *own* and manage the reference data.

For these reasons and more, reference data is often not managed with the same discipline that other data in the CIF is managed, yet it still requires as careful attention as any other type of data. There are at least two reasons why reference data plays a very important role in the world of the CIF:

1. Reference data is one of the primary ways in which different components of the CIF communicate and maintain continuity with each other. For example, if reference data in the applications environment is the same as reference data in the data warehouse, then the task of I & T is made much simpler. However, if the I & T layer must completely discard one approach to reference data and create an entirely brand new reference system (which can be done in extreme cases), then the logic of I & T processing becomes very complex and cumbersome. If there is consistency of reference data across the many different systems of the CIF, then the organization is one step closer to achieving an integrated environment.

2. Reference data ages over time. In the data warehouse, as reference data ages, a historical record must be kept so that the historical data that resides in the warehouse can have references made to data that is accurate as of the moment of the creation of the data warehouse record. In other words, because historical data is stored in the data warehouse, an historical reference needs to be kept. If the DSS analyst is going back to 1995 to look at data in the data warehouse, he needs to be able to know what the reference data was for 1995. It will not do to have the DSS analyst looking at 1995 data from the data warehouse where the DSS is trying to use reference tables from 1997. The need for historical referencibility is one of the important and peculiar needs of the data warehouse within the context of the CIF.

External Data

A key source of data found in the CIF is that of external data (Figure 2.3). External data is data originating outside the CIF. Typically, external data is purchased or created by another corporation. It can be of almost any type and volume, and can be either structured or unstructured, detailed or summarized. In short, there are as many types of external data as there are internal data.

One fundamental way in which external data differs from internal data is in its ability to be manipulated. When there is a need to change internal data, the programs that

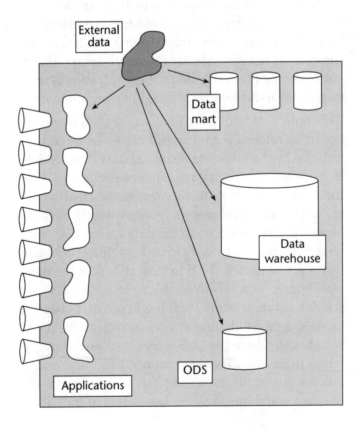

FIGURE 2.3

External data is an integral part of the CIF environment.

capture and shape it can always be altered. In that sense internal data is very malleable.

However, external data is pretty much *what you see is what you get*. Because the sources for the external data lie beyond the CIF, it is beyond the scope of the CIF architect to effect such a change in it. About the only real choice the CIF architect has to make is to either use the external data as is or to reject the usage of the external data altogether.

The one exception to the alteration of external data is that of modifying a key structure to the external data as it enters the CIF. This happens quite often when trying to match external data to an existing customer. Generally, an attempt is made to match the name and address associated to the external data, to a name and address in the customer database. If a match is made, the external key is replaced with the internal customer id and the external data is stored.

In many cases, the external data will have a key structure that is quite different from the key structure employed within the CIF. The external data needs to have its keys modified in order to be used meaningfully within the confines of the CIF.

The modification of the external key can be a simple or a difficult thing to accomplish. In some cases, the external key goes through a simple algorithm to convert it to the CIF key. In other cases, reference tables are used in conjunction with an algorithm. And in the worst case, the conversion is made manually, on a record-by-record basis. The manual approach to key resolution is not viable for massive amounts of data and/or where the manual conversion must be done repeatedly.

External data can be made available to any and all components of the CIF. If the external data is to be used in multiple data marts, it is a good policy to place the external data first in the data warehouse, then transport it individually to the data mart. By placing it first inside the data warehouse, reconcilability of the data is maintained.

Historical Data

Even when data has been entered into a computer system and it is ten seconds old, it is historical in the sense that it represents events now passed. Of course, the event that has passed is much more current than events that may have occurred a week ago or a month ago. Nevertheless, all data entered into a computer system can be thought of as historical data (with the exception of forecast data). The issue is not whether data is historical, but just how historical the data is. The implications of historical data are many, including:

- ❏ **Volume of data.** The longer the history is kept, the greater the amount of data.
- ❏ **Business usefulness.** The more current a unit of information, the greater the likelihood that it is relevant to current business.
- ❏ **Aggregation of data.** The more current the data, the greater the chance that the data will be used at the detailed level. The older the data, the greater the chance that the data will be used at the summary level.

There are many other implications of history. These are merely the obvious ones. Figure 2.4 shows that the components of the CIF contain different phases of corporate information history.

The applications environment contains very current information, up to 30 days. Of course, the actual time parameters vary across industries and businesses. Some industries may have more than 30 days worth of information; other industries may have less.

The ODS environment has a time period identical to that of the applications. The difference between the ODS and the applications is that the ODS contains integrated corporate data and the applications do not.

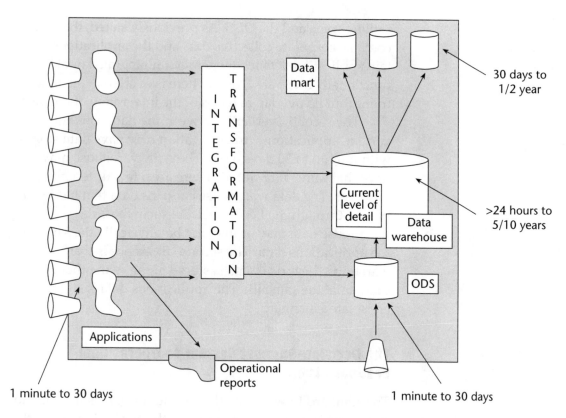

FIGURE 2.4
The amount of historical data that is found in the CIF differs from component to component.

The data warehouse contains data that is at least 24 hours old, up to 5 to 10 years worth of history. The actual length of time found here is highly dependent on the industry that is being represented by the data warehouse.

The data mart environment contains the widest variety of data found in the environment. The amount of history contained by a data mart is dependent on:

❏ The industry the corporation is in

❏ The company within the industry

❏ The department within the company

Of special interest is where there is an overlap between the different components. The first overlap is between the applications arena and the ODS. As previously stated, the ODS contains corporate collective data and the applications contain application detailed (generally unintegrated or at best functionally integrated) data. There is overlap in the time frame, but no overlap in terms of the integration of the data.

The second overlap is between the data warehouse and the applications. An application may have data stored within it, up to 30 days or so. The data warehouse may have that same data stored. There are a few differences, however. The data warehouse contains data that has been passed through the I & T layer. As such, the data warehouse data may or may not be physically the same as the applications data. The second difference is that the data warehouse historical data is stored along with other historical data of the same ilk. The applications data is stored in an isolated manner.

The Decision-Support System to Operational Feedback Loop

The standard flow of data throughout the CIF is from left to right, that is, from the consumer to the application, from the application to the I & T layer, from the I & T layer to the ODS or the data warehouse, from the ODS to the data warehouse, and from the data warehouse to the data marts. The flow occurs as described in a regular and normal manner. However, there is another feedback loop that is at work, as depicted in Figure 2.5.

Figure 2.5 shows that as data is used in the DSS (or informational) environment, decisions are made. As an example, a manager in the insurance environment decides to raise rates on a certain kind of policy based on the information derived from the DSS environment. Perhaps a bank manager decides to raise rates on car loans. Another example is a retailer deciding to produce more of product ABC based on strong demand detected in the DSS environment. In short, the DSS environment provides a basis for making business decisions.

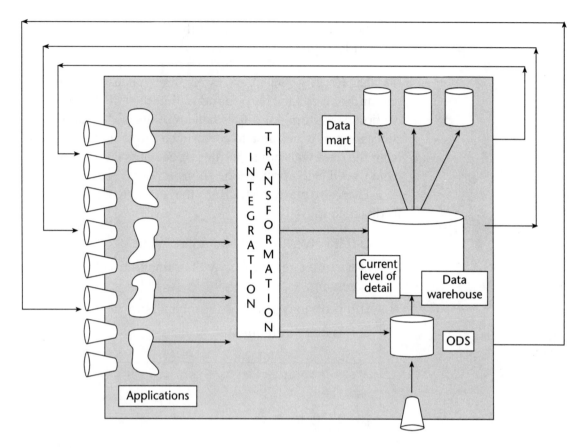

FIGURE 2.5
There is a feedback loop from the DSS/informational environment to the applications environment.

However, once those business decisions have been made, they have an impact which is first detected by the applications environment. For example, when the retailer decides to produce more of product ABC, sales are boosted across the United States and the increase in sales is measured by the applications systems having a direct inter-action with the consumer. Likewise, when an insurance executive decides to lower rates for a policy type, more policies are sold, which in turn is measured by the applications environment. In any case, the CIF operates as part of a holistic system. The ecosystem is regulated by the feedback loop shown in Figure 2.5. It is through this feedback loop that the different components of the CIF find a balance and constantly adjust to each other.

The Direct Feedback Loop   Very rarely, there is need for a different kind of feedback loop found within the CIF. On an exception basis done for only small amounts of data and processing, it is possible to construct a direct feedback loop from the data warehouse to the applications environment or from the ODS to applications environment (Figure 2.6).

There are many restrictions that apply to this direct feedback loop:

- ❏ It involves limited amounts of data.
- ❏ It cannot get in the way of online transaction processing.
- ❏ It is often is based on a probabilistic calculation.
- ❏ It is done infrequently.

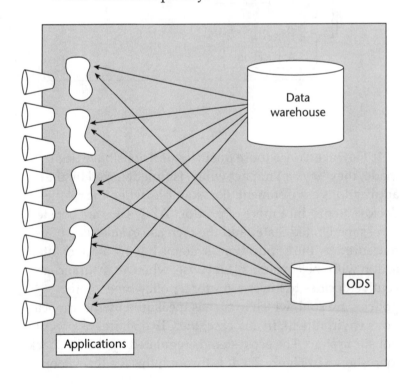

FIGURE 2.6

There is occasionally direct feedback from the ODS or the data warehouse to the applications environment. However, on those occasions when there is direct feedback along these channels, the feedback is restricted.

In spite of the restrictions of a direct feedback loop from the DSS to the application environment, on those occasions when such a feedback loop becomes useful, it really becomes useful. This is particularly the case when trying to deploy a new business process that requires availability and performance outside the current capabilities of the applications environment. In this scenario, the business request would be staged in the operational data store and the end-user would be free to continue with the next request. The job of the ODS would be to guarantee delivery of the request to the targeted application. If the request failed, the end-user would be notified.

VARIATIONS TO THE CORPORATE INFORMATION FACTORY

One of the common and valid variations to the corporate information factory occurs when there is no ODS. The ODS is peculiar in that many organizations find that they do not need an ODS to run their business. An ODS can be:

❏ Expensive and difficult to build

❏ Expensive to operate

❏ Challenging to maintain

There must be a very sound business case for an ODS. Of course, when an ODS is needed, there is nothing to replace it. Typically, businesses that are large businesses that require product integration, and businesses that do a lot of high-performance transaction processing are candidates for an ODS.

Because many corporations operate successfully without an ODS, one valid variation of the classical corporate information factory architecture, as shown in Figure 2.1, is an architecture where there is no ODS. When there is no ODS, the flow of all data is from the integration and transformation layer directly to the data warehouse.

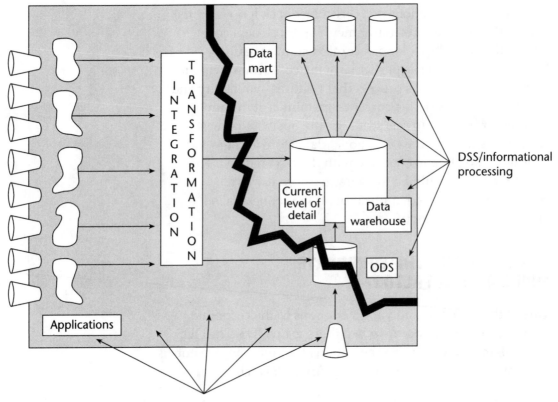

Operational transaction processing

FIGURE 2.7

There is a clean and clear cut separation between DSS/informational processing and operational processing in the corporate information factory.

OPERATIONAL PROCESSING AND DSS PROCESSING

There is a line where operational processing ends and DSS/informational processing begins. Figure 2.7 depicts that demarcation. The figure shows that the applications environment is entirely in the world of operational processing. Data marts and the data warehouse are completely in the world of DSS/informational processing. The ODS sits squarely in the middle of the world of informational and operational processing. With an ODS, there is both operational and informational processing in the same structure. This is one of the reasons why the ODS is the most complex part of the information ecosystem. Every other part of the infrastructure can be optimized to suit one style of processing or the other. But the ODS must be optimal (or at least acceptable!) for more than one style of processing. This factor greatly complicates the life of the builder and the manager of the ODS environment.

REPORTING IN THE CORPORATE INFORMATION FACTORY

Analysis of data and reporting can be done throughout the corporate information factory. There is no point at which data is locked up and becomes unavailable. But at each different component of the architecture, the reporting that is done is quite different. The different kinds of reporting are:

❏ Operational reporting—ODS reporting for collective integrated data
❏ Data warehouse reporting
❏ Data mart departmental reporting

Each of the types of reporting has its own unique characteristics.

CORPORATE INFORMATION FACTORY USERS

There are different types of users who access the corporate information factory at different places. Figure 2.8 shows the typical users of the application level of the corporate information factory.

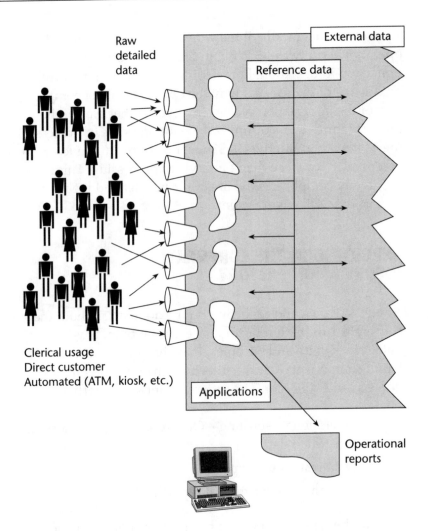

Raw
detailed
data

External data

Reference data

Clerical usage
Direct customer
Automated (ATM, kiosk, etc.)

Applications

Operational
reports

FIGURE 2.8
*The users of the applications
are very detail-oriented and
concerned with up-to-the-
second accurate information.*

Applications Users

The users of applications are primarily from the clerical or
sales/service professional and, in some cases, the customers
of the corporation themselves. Occasionally, the customers
have direct interaction with the corporate applications
through facilities such as ATMs, kiosks, and even through
direct entry using their personal computer. In other cases, a
clerk is required to enter detailed data taken from the cus-

tomer. The kind of data that is handled at the application level is:

Detailed

Immediate

Application-oriented

The user of the technology at the application level can expect immediate feedback in the form of transactions. High-performance transactions are the order here with two-to-three second response time as the norm. There is a high degree of availability across the network that supports the application.

The nature of the applications in the corporate information factory includes:

❏ Interacting with the end user
❏ Collecting data
❏ Editing data
❏ Auditing data
❏ Allowing adjustments and corrections to be made
❏ Verifying transactions
❏ Keeping an accurate record of events
❏ Keeping online data accurate with a high degree of integrity
❏ Allowing small units of data to be accessed very rapidly
❏ Securing data and transactions, etc.

The interaction with the end users at the application level is through reports and terminals (usually preprogrammed, tightly controlled *dumb terminals*). The applications have their own store of data which is augmented by reference data and external data. As a rule, the applications environment is unintegrated, where each application serves a particular need and a unique set of requirements.

Decision-Support System/Informational Users

DSS/informational users are very different from operational users. They are solving or investigating longer-term questions. Operational users are concerned with very immediate and very direct decisions, such as:

- ❑ How much money is in an account right now?
- ❑ Where is a shipment right now?
- ❑ What coverage is there for a policy right now?
- ❑ When is an order due?

DSS users are concerned with decisions that are much broader and long term, such as:

- ❑ What type of customer is the most profitable for our corporation?
- ❑ Over the years, how has transaction activity changed?
- ❑ Where has sales activity been highest in the springtime for the past three years?
- ❑ When we change prices, how much elasticity is there in the marketplace?

The DSS analysts have a whole different perspective on the use and value of information. They look at:

- ❑ Information that has been integrated across the corporation
- ❑ Broad vistas of information, instead of small divisions of information

❏ Information over a lengthy period of time, rather
than very current data

There are some very different characteristics between
the usage of information by DSS analysts and operational
analysts, such as:

❏ The DSS analyst often looks at very large amounts of
information as opposed to the operational analyst
who looks at tiny bits of information.

❏ The DSS analyst does not need to have information
returned immediately. Five minutes, 30 minutes, or
even overnight in many cases is just fine for the DSS
analyst, as opposed to the operational analyst who
needs two- to three-seconds response time.

In addition, the very way that information is sought is different between the DSS analyst and the operational analyst.
The DSS analyst looks for information heuristically, where
the next step of analysis is profoundly shaped by the results
obtained in the previous step of analysis, and where the
exact shape or even the extent of an analysis cannot be determined at the outset.

The operational analyst operates in a mode where
queries and questions are preformatted into a very structured format. The same activity is repeated over and over
again, where all that changes is the data that is being operated on in the world of the operational user. Figure 2.9
shows that there are many different kinds of DSS analysts.

At the departmental level there are data mart analysts
who do decision support through the eyes of their department. Typical departments are finance, marketing, and
sales. The customized summary data that is found in the
data mart is exactly what the data mart analyst needs to
satisfy the peculiar needs of data mart DSS processing.

Exploratory analysis is done at the data warehouse.

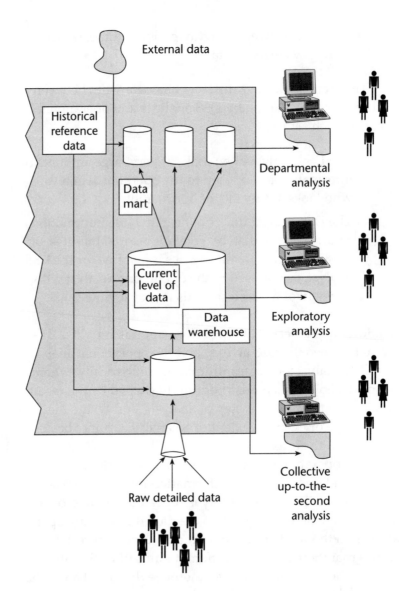

FIGURE 2.9

DSS/informational users are very different from operational users.

The integrated, detailed data and the robust amount of history found at the data warehouse are ideal for this type of analysis.

Collective integrated operational analysis can be done at the ODS. Admittedly, much true operational processing is done at the ODS. But occasionally there is a need to do operational DSS processing. When that need arises, the ODS is the ideal place for processing.

There are different types of DSS users scattered throughout the corporate information factory. The three most common types of DSS users are tourists, farmers, and explorers.

Tourists   Tourists are those DSS analysts who specialize in being able to find a breadth of information, as illustrated in Figure 2.10.

In the figure, a tourist is seen as an individual who uses the Internet and knows where to find many things. A tourist understands the structure of the corporate information factory and knows where in the structure of things to find almost anything. However, the tourist is an unpredictable analyst, sort of a walking directory of information.

Tourists

- Look over lots of data on a random basis
- Often never look over the same data twice
- Do not know what the requirements are
- Make heavy use of metadata
- Occasionally stumble on something that proves to be useful
- Uses Internet regularly
- Monitor beds of data regularly
- Look over huge amounts of data on a regular basis
- Sporadic usage of data
- Heavy reliance on tools for scanning
- Sometimes find arenas for further exploration

FIGURE 2.10
One type of DSS user is the Tourist.

Farmers   A farmer is a very different kind of DSS analyst than a tourist, as shown in Figure 2.11.

This figure shows a farmer as someone who is predictable and knows what he or she wants before setting out to do a query. A farmer looks at small amounts of data because the farmer knows where to find the data. The farmer is somewhat repetitive in the search for information and seldom wanders far from data that is familiar. The farmer operates as comfortably on detailed data as on summary data. In many regards, because summary data is compact and concise, summary data suits the needs of the farmer quite nicely. In addition, the data the farmer is looking for is almost always here.

Farmers

- Regular access to data
- Know what they are looking for
- Access small amounts of data
- Predictable access to data
- Predictable processing once data accessed
- Requirements known before search for data starts
- Access data marts regularly
- Unusual to access current level of detail
- Find small flakes of gold regularly
- Make use of tools of presentation

FIGURE 2.11

A second type of DSS user is a Farmer.

Explorers   A third type of DSS analyst is someone known as an explorer, as shown in Figure 2.12.

The figure shows that the explorers have some traits similar to both the tourist and the farmer, but are unique unto themselves. The explorer is someone who operates with a great degree of unpredictability and irregularity, and looks over massive amounts of detail. The explorer seldom has much use for summary data and frequently makes requests that seem to be farfetched. Often times the explorer finds nothing, but occasionally the explorer finds huge nuggets in the most unexpected places. The explorer becomes an expert in one arena within the corporate information factory.

Explorers

- Irregular access to data
- Does not know what they are looking for
- Look over masses of data
- Unpredictable pattern of access
- Sometimes find huge nuggets
- Often find nothing
- Requirements are totally unknown
- Access current level detail regularly
- Look at relationships of data rather than occurrences of data
- Make use of tools of discovery and statistical analysis and exploration

FIGURE 2.12
A third type of DSS user is an Explorer.

Types of DSS Usage in the Corporate Information Factory Environment

Understanding that there are different kinds of DSS users with very different goals and techniques is the first step in resolving many seemingly complex and contradictory facets of the corporate information factory. Without this perspective, many DSS components of the corporate information factory do not make sense.

As an example of the perspective provided, consider that different parts of the DSS environment within the corporate information factory attract and apply to different types of users, as seen in Figure 2.13.

The figure shows that data mart and departmental analysis apply to farmers and the occasional tourist. Explorers are attracted to the data warehouse and, once in a while, the tourist finds his or her way into the data warehouse. The ODS environment is almost exclusively the domain of farmers. It is worthwhile noting that the farmers found at the ODS environment are quite different from the farmers found at the data mart. The data mart farmers are those people who are analyzing a problem for possible future action. The farmers at the ODS environment are those who are interested in an immediate short-term tactical corporate decision, not some long-term consideration. For example, is this customer a good credit risk?

One of the reasons why the separation of the DSS analyst community into different audiences is important is that it explains why there are such diverse design and development practices throughout the DSS portion of the corporate information factory.

CENTRALIZED OR DISTRIBUTED?

One of the most important issues of the corporate information factory is whether the underlying component of the architecture is (under normal circumstances) centralized or

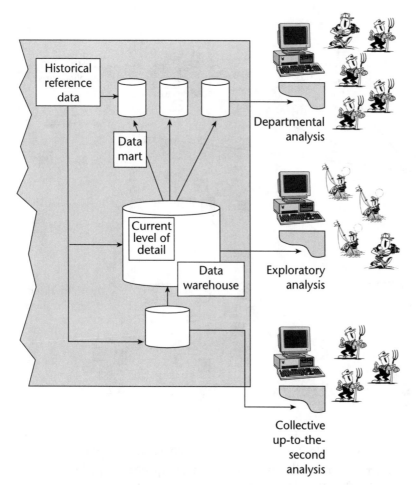

Historical reference data

Data mart

Current level of detail

Data warehouse

Departmental analysis

Exploratory analysis

Collective up-to-the-second analysis

FIGURE 2.13
Different types of usage occur at different levels within the DSS/informational portion of the corporate factory.

distributed. This issue is salient to the implementation, functionality, and economics of the ultimate deployment of the corporate information factory. It needs to be considered on a case-by-case basis for each of the different components of the architecture. Figure 2.14 addresses centralization of the applications environment.

Since the applications environment can be either centralized or distributed, the decision is usually made by history: The hardware, and the past development and deployment of the application environment determine whether the applications are centralized or distributed.

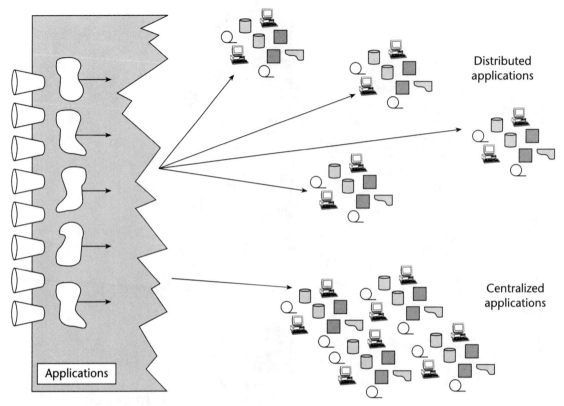

FIGURE 2.14
Applications can either be distributed or centralized.

As a rule, large transaction-processing applications are centralized, while smaller off-line, sequential applications tend to be distributed. The ODS is almost always centralized, as seen in Figure 2.15.

While in theory it may be possible to have a distributed ODS environment, in practice all ODS are centralized.

The data warehouse is another matter. The data warehouse can be either centralized or distributed, as shown in Figure 2.16.

In general, most data warehouses are centralized. But there are some very notable and successful examples of distributed data warehouses. These have a slightly different form from a classic centralized data warehouse. When a data warehouse is distributed, the detail of the system is left

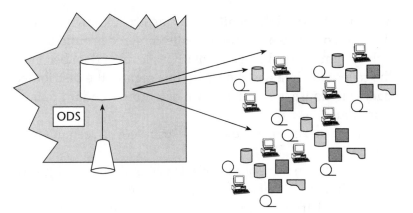

FIGURE 2.15
The ODS is almost always centralized.

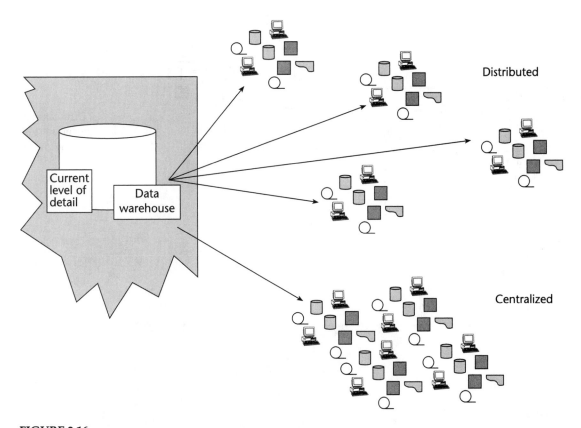

Distributed

Centralized

FIGURE 2.16
The data warehouse can either be distributed or centralized. The normal case is that it is centralized.

at the local level. The architectural construct known as the distributed data warehouse is really centered around a lightly summarized level of data. This level of data becomes the corporate data warehouse. In this regard, the distributed data warehouse is a mutant form of a more standard data warehouse.

Data marts are exclusively distributed, as seen in Figure 2.17.

The very nature of data marts is that they be unique to the environment that owns or controls them. As such, data marts are distributed around the different departments of the corporation in many shapes and forms.

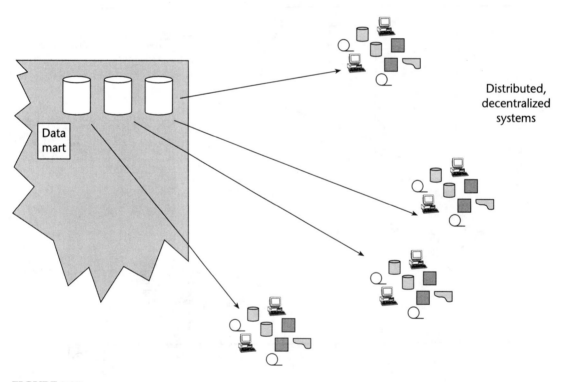

Distributed, decentralized systems

FIGURE 2.17
The data mart environment is distributed and decentralized.

DATA MODELING AND THE CORPORATE INFORMATION FACTORY

The corporate information factory has many disparate parts. While there is an overall dynamic to the corporate information factory, each component has its own parts and internal interactions. Therefore, there needs to be some mechanism or technique that allows the corporate information factory to function in a coordinated, cohesive manner. The structure of the different components is unified by means of a data model. The data model allows each of the architectural components of the corporate information factory to have as much autonomy as it needs, and at the same time allows the corporate information factory to operate in a unified manner. The data model is the data blueprint and intellectually unifies the data warehouse. Figure 2.18 shows the role of the data model to the corporate information factory.

The data model exists for the entire organization and plays a different role for each of the architectural components in the corporate information factory. The data model:

❏ Serves as a guide for the ongoing reconstruction of the applications environment. Since the applications environment is notoriously unintegrated, the data model serves as a basis for bringing together the different applications as they are rewritten or as they are modified.

❏ Is the basis for subject-area design for both the ODS and the data warehouse. The general structuring of the ODS and the data warehouse begins with an orientation towards the major subject areas of the corporation. The orientation corresponds precisely to the entities that are defined in the high-level logical data model.

But the corporate data model does not directly serve the needs of the departments that have data marts. The de-

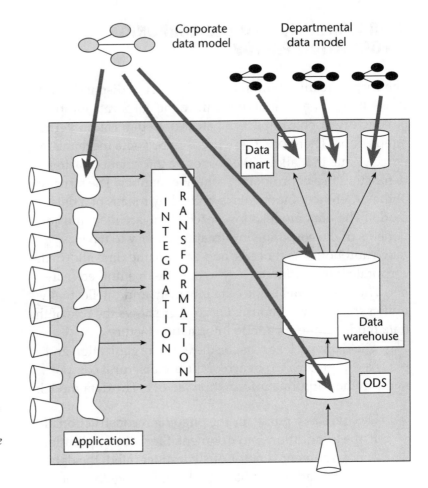

FIGURE 2.18

The data model(s) forms the basis of the structure of the different components of the architecture. The data marts are shaped by individual data models; the other architectural components are shaped by the corporate data model.

partmental data marts are patterned after the requirements that apply to and are unique to a particular department. As a rule, the departmental data model is a subset of or is profoundly shaped by the corporate data model.

Because all departments are a smaller part of a larger whole, there is an indirect relationship between the corporate data model and the individual departmental data models that shapes the design of the various data marts.

MIGRATING TO THE CORPORATE INFORMATION FACTORY

The size and complexity of the corporate information factory dictates that the fully mature architecture be achieved a step at a time. For all practical purposes, it is impossible to build the corporate information factory all at once. In fact, there are many good reasons to support a step-at-a-time approach to the building of the corporate information factory, such as:

❏ **Cost.** The cost of the infrastructure and the cost of development are simply prohibitive to consider the building of the corporate information factory at anything but a step at a time.

❏ **Complexity.** The corporate information factory entails the usage of many different kinds of technologies. An organization can absorb only so many technologies at once.

❏ **Nature of the environment.** The DSS portion of the environment is built iteratively in any case. It does not make sense to build the DSS environment in a "big bang" approach.

❏ **Value.** Above all else, the implementation of the corporate information factory must demonstrate incremental value to the business. This is best accomplished through a series of three- to six-month iterations.

For these reasons the corporate information factory emerges from the information systems of a corporation over time, not all at once.

There is a typical progression to the building of the corporate information factory, as shown in Figure 2.19–2.20.

The figure shows that on Day 1 there is a chaotic information systems environment that is without shape and

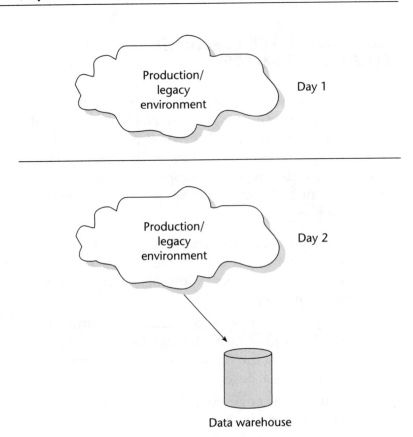

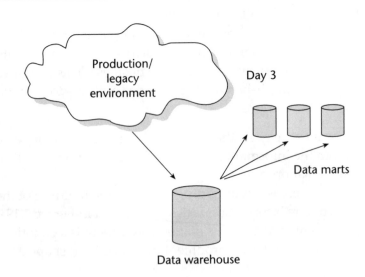

FIGURE 2.19

The typical first three steps to the movement to the corporate information factory from the production/legacy environment.

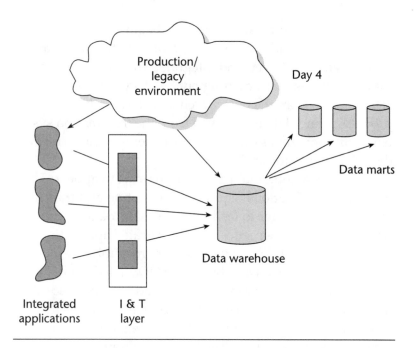

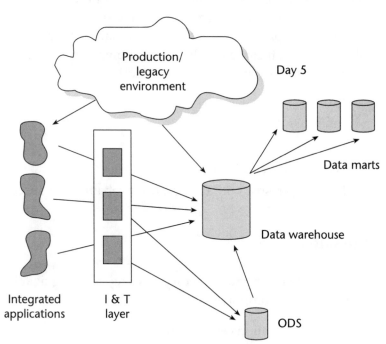

FIGURE 2.20
Migrating to the corporate information factory—latter phases.

form. On Day 2, the data warehouse begins to emerge and grows incrementally. With each advance in the data warehouse, data is removed and integrated from the amorphous information systems environment. On Day 3, data marts start to grow from the data warehouse. Indirectly, more processing and data is removed from the information systems environment as different departments begin to rely on their data marts for DSS processing.

On Day 4, integrated applications start to appear. The integrated applications require an integration and transformation layer in order to feed the data to the data warehouse. The emergence of the integrated applications comes slowly and, in many cases, imperceptibly.

On Day 5, the ODS is built. The ODS is fed from the integration and transformation layer and, in turn, feeds its data to the data warehouse. By this time the systems that were once known as the production systems environment have almost disappeared. The legacy environment is only a very small vestige of its former invincible self.

There are plenty of other migration paths that are possible other than the one that has been shown. However, the path that has been suggested is one that is:

Proven

Least risky

Fastest

Avoids many pitfalls

Least expensive with the greatest probability of success

SUMMARY

The corporate information factory has several recognizable and predictable components:

❏ An applications environment

❏ An integration and transformation layer

❑ An ODS

❑ A data warehouse

❑ Multiple data marts

❑ An Internet and intranet for providing the necessary intercommunications

❑ A metadata repository

The applications play the role of gathering raw data from interaction with customers. The applications level is a transaction-processing environment.

The ODS environment is the place where collective, corporate online operational integration occurs. The ODS is the most challenging environment to build and operate because it sometimes needs to support both informational and operational processing.

The data warehouse is where historical integrated information for the corporation is stored. The data warehouse typically contains huge amounts of data and represents the essence of corporate data.

Data marts exist for the many different departments that need to do DSS processing. Data marts are a customized, summarized subset of the data that resides in the data warehouse.

The world of the CIF is split along the lines of operational processing and DSS/informational processing. Applications belong in the domain of operational processing. Data marts and data warehouse are clearly in the DSS/informational world. The ODS is split into informational and operational aspects.

The community of DSS users can be divided into three classifications: tourists, explorers, and farmers. Each of the different classifications of DSS users has its own distinct set of characteristics.

There is a standard progression from the classical production, legacy environment to the corporate information factory. First, the data warehouse is built; next the data marts are built; and finally, the ODS is built, if the ODS is built at all. Many corporations do not need an ODS.

So far, we have talked about the *heart* of the information ecosystem, the corporate information factory. In the next chapter, we will talk about the most prominent component of the CIF, the data warehouse.

3

The Data Warehouse Component

T he most prominent architectural component of the corporate information factory is that of the data warehouse. It
is the basis for all strategic DSS processing. In many cases,
the data warehouse is the first place integration of data is
achieved anywhere in the environment. It is also where
much historical processing is done.

WHAT IS THE DATA WAREHOUSE?

The data warehouse is an architectural structure that supports the management of data that is:

- ❏ Subject-oriented
- ❏ Integrated
- ❏ Time-variant
- ❏ Non-volatile
- ❏ Contains both summary and detailed data

51

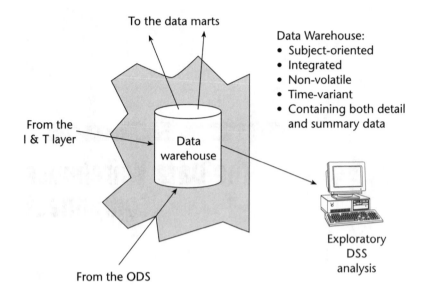

To the data marts

Data Warehouse:
• Subject-oriented
• Integrated
• Non-volatile
• Time-variant
• Containing both detail and summary data

From the
I & T layer

Data
warehouse

Exploratory
DSS
analysis

From the ODS

FIGURE 3.1
A data warehouse in the context of the corporate information factory.

The data warehouse exists to support management's decisions which, in turn, support the strategic planning processes of the corporation. Data flows into the data warehouse from the ODS and the I & T layer. The flow of data out of the data warehouse goes to the data marts. Finally, there are DSS analysts who use the data found in the data mart to support such activities as customer profiling, market segmentation, product analysis, and projecting customer lifetime value. Figure 3.1 illustrates the data warehouse in the context of the corporate information factory.

Subject Orientation

The subject orientation of the data warehouse implies that it is organized along the lines of the major entities of the corporation, such as:

Customers
Products
Vendors

Transactions

Orders

Policies

Accounts

Shipments

In other words, the data warehouse is not functionally or application oriented. This allows for the use of data to change over time without fundamentally affecting its organization or structure. This is crucial given the large volumes of historical data that are managed within the data warehouse.

Integration

Integration of data warehouse data refers to the physical unification and cohesiveness of the data as it is stored in the warehouse. Integration covers many aspects of the warehouse, including:

❏ Common key structures

❏ Common encoding and decoding structures

❏ Common definitions of data

❏ Common data layouts

❏ Common data relationships

❏ Common naming conventions

Integration of data in the data warehouse is not achieved by merely copying data from the operational environment. Instead, as raw data passes through the I & T layer, a fundamental alteration is done to the data to achieve an integrated foundation that resides in the data warehouse.

Time Variancy

Another characteristic of a data warehouse is that of time variancy. Simply stated, any record in the data warehouse environment is accurate relative to some moment in time. One way time variancy is accomplished is through the creation of snapshot records. A data warehouse is often said to contain nothing but a massive series of snapshot records. Each snapshot has one moment in time when the record is accurate. Any implication about the record before or beyond the moment in time that the snapshot was made is misleading and may be inaccurate.

Because the data warehouse is made up of a massive series of snapshots, it can contain data over a lengthy period of time. It is not uncommon for a data warehouse to hold detail data (active or archival) that is 5 to 10 years old.

The time variancy of a data warehouse shows up as an element of time in the key structure. An element of time might be a day, a year, a month, or a quarter. The element of time is appended to the key of the record in the data warehouse. There are two popular models used in recording history, State and Event. A record using a State model has a "from" and "to" date that denotes the time period when the data in the record was accurate. An example of this is:

> Customer id
>
> From date
>
> To date

A record using the Event model has an "event" date that reflects the moment in time when the data in the record was accurate. Two examples of this are:

> Order id
> Part number
> Order date

and

> Account withdrawal id
> Withdrawal date

Non-Volatility

Yet another characteristic of a data warehouse is that of non-volatility. This refers to the fact that update (in its purest sense—that of finding a record and making changes to the record) does not normally occur in a data warehouse. If update occurs at all, it occurs on an exception basis.

When changes occur that need to be recorded in a data warehouse, the changes are captured in the form of a time-variant snapshot. A new snapshot is added to the data warehouse to reflect the change instead of an update occurring. In capturing change by means of a series of snapshots, a historical record is formed.

Containment of Summary and Detailed Data

Finally, a data warehouse contains both detailed and summary data. Detailed data reflects the atomic-level transactions that turn the wheels of the corporation. This includes data that describes customers, product usage, account activity, inventory movement, sales, and so forth. There are two kinds of summary data found in a data warehouse: the profile record and public summary data.

The Profile Record   One kind of summary data is created as raw detailed data in the I & T layer and combined to create a profile or aggregate record. As an example of a profile record, consider the following example from the telecommunications industry.

In the operational environment there is a customer record and a record for each use of the telephone during the statement cycle. Throughout the statement cycle many usage records are created. When it comes time to create a data warehouse record at the end of the statement cycle, the usage transaction records are combined to create a single record which is then placed in the data warehouse. The resultant record is an aggregate or profile record that contains summary data representing the lowest level of granularity of data warehouse data. This form of summary data—a transaction summary record —in the data warehouse is common for organizations dealing with very large amounts of data in their data warehouse. Typically, those organizations include:

> Telecommunications providers
> Retailers
> Insurance companies
> Financial institutions

Public Summary Data   The second type of summary data found in the data warehouse is a type of data that can be termed *public summary*. It reflects data that is calculated departmentally but has wide corporate outreach. An example of a public summary is the calculation made each quarter by the public accounting firm stating the financial status of the corporation. The quarterly statement includes such things as expenses, revenues, and profitability. The financial status reflects benchmark information that is used across the corporation by many departments and many managers. While the quarterly statement is prepared departmentally, it is used throughout the corporation, and as such is an example of public summary data. As a proportion of data, public summary data occupies a minuscule amount of space in the data warehouse compared to detail or profile summary data.

DATA WAREHOUSE ADMINISTRATION

As a rule, the data warehouse is managed by an organizational unit called a data warehouse administrator or DWA. The DWA organization has many charters, such as:

❑ Building the data warehouse

❏ Ongoing monitoring and maintenance for the data warehouse

❏ Coordinating usage of the data warehouse

❏ Management feedback as to successes and failures

❏ Competition for resources for making the data warehouse a reality

❏ Selection of hardware and software platforms

THE DATA WAREHOUSE DRAWN TO SCALE

One interesting way to look at the data warehouse as it sits in the corporate information factory is to look at it drawn to scale, as shown in Figure 3.2.

As the figure indicates, the data warehouse, in terms of data and processing, is much larger than any other component of the corporate information factory. As a rule (and this depends entirely on the company and its experience with the data warehouse), the data warehouse is one to one and a half

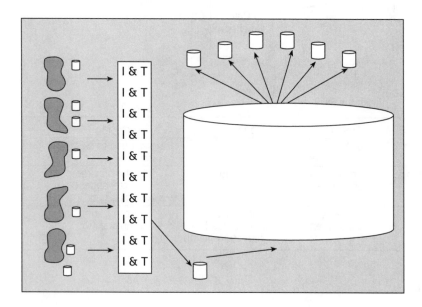

FIGURE 3.2

The data warehouse drawn to scale in comparison with the other components of the corporate information factory.

orders of magnitude larger than any other architectural component. Of course, if an organization is just embarking on the data warehouse and there is very little experience in this environment, then the data warehouse will be proportionately smaller than that shown in Figure 3.2. The ratios depicted in Figure 3.2 are for a mature data warehouse environment.

FEEDS INTO AND OUT OF THE DATA WAREHOUSE

The data warehouse has data moved into it from the ODS and the I & T layer. In addition, the data warehouse feeds the data mart environment; each of the feeds has its own characteristics. Figure 3.3 shows the feeds of data into and out of the data warehouse.

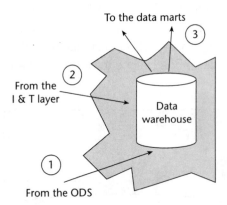

	Volume	Timing	Mode	Processing
1. From the ODS	Very light	daily	Mass load	Append to existing data
2. From the I & T layer	Very heavy	At night; on an as-needed basis	Mass load	Replace; incremental update; append to existing data
3. To data marts	Moderate	Varies by department	Selective or mass unload with aggregation	Customization and summarization

FIGURE 3.3
The different feeds to and from the data warehouse.

The Operational Data Store Feed

The ODS feed is one in which very little data is passed to the data warehouse; it is triggered by data aging in the ODS. The ODS feed is usually made daily and typically brings data into the data warehouse where that data is appended to other data in the warehouse. Since a small amount of data is moved from the ODS to the data warehouse, an intranet connection is very effective.

Often times data is aggregated as it is moved out of the ODS and into the data warehouse. The programs that comprise the ODS to data warehouse interface are the domain of the DWA. Any other organizational unit having influence over this interface does not make sense.

The Integration and Transformation Layer Feed

The movement of data into the data warehouse from the I & T layer is one where there is a massive amount of data crossing the line. The intranet connection must be capable of handling very large amounts of data transfer.

The I & T connection is one that is executed on an as-needed basis. Sometimes transfer is made daily, sometimes transfer is made weekly, and occasionally transfer is made monthly or even quarterly. In any case, huge amounts of data regularly cross from the I & T layer into the data warehouse. The transfer is made on a casual basis in that there is no implication that a high-speed online update will be done once the data arrives at the data warehouse. The nature of update into the data warehouse is one of replace, or addition.

Data can be passed in either an aggregated or detailed form into the data warehouse from the I & T layer. Note that the data that arrives in the data warehouse is often very changed from its original form and structure as it has left the application. The data that arrives in the data warehouse through the I & T layer is data that has undergone transformation. Because of this, the data usually has been altered: In some cases, the alteration has been severe; in other cases, the alteration has been superficial, depending on just how integrated the data was to begin with.

Entering the Data Warehouse   The movement of data into the data warehouse is the last part of the I & T layer. As such, the programs are written and controlled by the DWA organization. It is very unusual for any other organizational entity to be involved with the specification and creation of the programs that comprise the I & T feed into the data warehouse other than the DWA.

Feeds into the Data Mart

Data moves into the data mart environment because it has been selected by the department for its own unique DSS processing. The data mart interface can be characterized as customization and summarization.

The department selects data from the data warehouse on an as-needed basis. In almost all cases, the department will not want the lengthy amount of detail history that is found in the data warehouse and it will want to customize the data. The ultimate degree of customization will be heavily influenced by the business use and the DSS tool selected. Customization often includes:

❏ Restructuring the keys
❏ Resequencing the data
❏ Merging files together
❏ Aggregating data (creating corporate *profiles*)
❏ Denormalizing data

The volume of data that flows across this portion of the intranet is actually very slight, compared to other interfaces.

There are, of course, different ports for different data

marts. There is no need for the sales department to share the same port into the data warehouse with marketing, for example. Likewise, the frequency of the movement of data across the feed is strictly based on the needs of the department.

As a rule, the department builds and administers the programs that control the data warehouse to data mart interface. Only if there are extenuating circumstances is it necessary or advisable to bring a DWA programmer in to create and manage the programs for the interface. However, the department may want to look to the DWA for advice on how to best extract data from the data warehouse.

DATA IN THE DATA WAREHOUSE

There is a large volume of detailed data in the data warehouse (Figure 3.4). For the most part, any summary data does not entail significant amounts of data. Data in the warehouse is integrated, so that it is distinctively corporate data. There is a rich amount of history of data in the data warehouse, from 5 to 10 years worth. As previously mentioned, the data is structured in terms of snapshots, which may be direct or aggregate snapshots. The snapshots may be for an instant in time or for a continuous amount of time.

The design for the data found in the data warehouse is dominated by normalized design. This technique, introduced by E. F. Codd, consists of a series of normalization rules that define the enterprise data in terms of:

- ❏ **Entities.** Things of interest (e.g., customer, product, etc.)
- ❏ **Attributes.** Elements that describe the things of interest (e.g., customer name, product type, etc.)
- ❏ **Relationships.** That describe the relationship among entities (e.g., a customer could have one or more products)

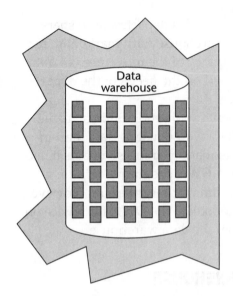

- Detailed
- Integrated
- Voluminous
- Historical
- Not updated (snapshots)
- Single snapshots and profile records
- Dominated by normalization

FIGURE 3.4
Data in the data warehouse.

This design technique strived to eliminate data redundancy and produce a stable database design that would be largely unaffected as the processes of the business changed. Though some denormalization does take place to address the performance demands of the business, the design is essentially one that is normalized. Any redundancy of data found in the data warehouse design is planned and minimal.

PROCESSING DATA IN THE WAREHOUSE

The processing in the data warehouse comes in five distinct flavors:

1. Loads from the ODS and the I & T layer into the data warehouse.
2. Processes to perform post-load aggregations and derivations (e.g., scoring & segmentation).
3. Utilities required to maintain and operate the data warehouse.

4. Unload processes to create data marts.

5. Some query processing from the DSS analyst community.

Maintenance and operational utilities occasionally must be run that:

❑ Monitor the amount of data that is being added to the data warehouse

❑ Monitor the quality of data that has been entered into the data warehouse

❑ Create a data content card catalog that tells what the content of the data warehouse is and projects future growth

❑ Prepare the data for recovery in the eventuality that there should be a problem with the data

❑ Remove data from the data warehouse

❑ Create indexes

In short, there are a number of background utilities that are required for the running of any data warehouse.

The more interesting programs that must be run are those that are submitted by the DSS analyst, illustrated in Figure 3.5.

Using the analogy of tourists, farmers, and explorers introduced in Chapter 2, the DSS analyst who operates directly on the data warehouse is usually an explorer. Only when the data warehouse is in its early days and there is a modest amount of data in the warehouse is it feasible for general-purpose DSS analysis to be done directly from the warehouse. Once the warehouse reaches a state of maturity and contains a serious volume of data, the analysis that is done is almost exclusively by an explorer. Farmers and tourists simply have little or no use for the warehouse once it matures.

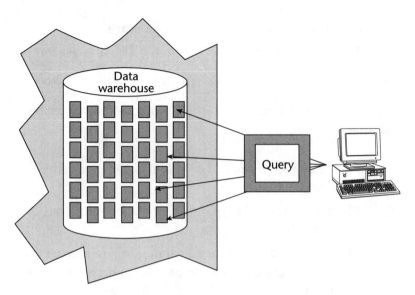

- Exploratory processing
- Looking at massive amounts of data
- Nonrepetitive
- Unpredictable
- Non-mission-critical
- Response time insensitive
- Browsing is common
- Unknown relationships are sometimes of interest
- Obscure data elements sometimes play an important role

FIGURE 3.5
DSS processing in the data warehouse.

The explorer typically looks for massive amounts of detailed data, in a very nonrepetitive manner and the searches conducted are not mission-critical. The processing that occurs is response-time insensitive; that is, response time may be measured in minutes, hours, or even days. Browsing is a common activity, looking at relationships of data and units of data that may be obscure.

MANAGING TECHNOLOGICAL CHALLENGES

The major technological challenges facing the DWA are depicted by the information in Figure 3.6.

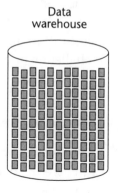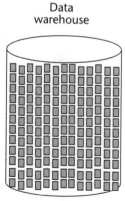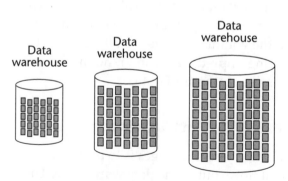

Growth is the first technological challenge
of the data warehouse environment.

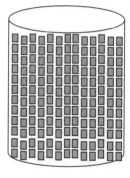

Volumes of data are the second
technological challenge.

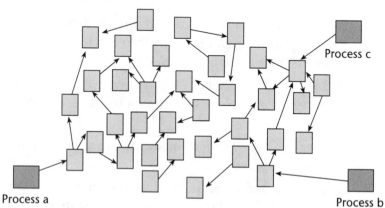

Process c

Process a

Process b

Processes that look at data in a completely unpredictable fashion, where
there is no predictability of processing.

FIGURE 3.6

Some of the more important technological challenges of the data warehouse environment.

The first and most important technological challenge facing the DWA is that of managing growth. Hand in hand is the issue of managing the volumes of data. Finally, there is the challenge of managing unpredictable and random access, and analysis of massive amounts of data.

Archiving Data out of the Data Warehouse

One way of addressing these challenges is to properly archive the data that flows out of the data warehouse. The data warehouse has a large volume of data flowing into it, but, like all databases there is no such thing as a database that constantly grows larger. At some point in time, it is necessary to purge or condense data out of the data warehouse. Figure 3.7 shows data being moved out of the data warehouse into siloed sequential storage, a typical approach.

There are many considerations to the movement of data out of the data warehouse, such as:

❏ Should the data be actually discarded or should the data be removed to lower-cost, bulk storage?

❏ What criteria should be applied to data to determine whether it is a candidate for removal?

❏ Should the data be condensed (profile records, rolling summarization, etc.)? If so, what condensation technique should be used?

❏ How should the data be indexed once it is removed (if there is ever to be any attempt to retrieve the data)?

❏ Where and how should metadata be stored once the data is removed?

❏ Should metadata be allowed to be stored in the data warehouse for data that is not actively stored in the warehouse?

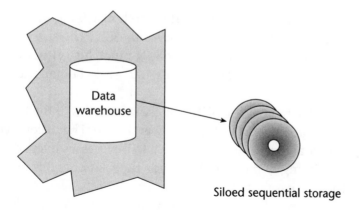

FIGURE 3.7
An integral part of the data warehouse environment is the occasional archiving of data out of active storage.

❑ What release information should be stored for the base technology (i.e., the DBMS) so that the data as stored will not become stale and unreadable?

❑ How reliable (physically) is the media that the data will be stored on?

❑ What seek time to first record is there for the data upon retrieval?

These are but a few of the questions that must be answered when deciding upon an exit strategy for the data that resides on the data warehouse. Most organizations do not spend much time thinking about these strategies until the data warehouse has become robust and mature.

SUMMARY

The data warehouse is at the heart of corporate data and DSS processing. It is fed by the ODS and the I & T layer and, in turn, feeds the data marts. In addition, some direct analysis—primarily by explorers—is done at the data warehouse itself.

Drawn to scale, the data warehouse is significantly larger than other components of the CIF. The size of the warehouse is determined by how much historical data is to be contained within it and at what level of detail the data is to be stored.

There are very different characteristics of the feeds of data into and out of the data warehouse. The differences center around the volume of data that passes over the feed, the timing of the feed, the mode the feed operates in, and the processing that occurs as a result of the feed.

Some of the more important technological challenges of the data warehouse center around the management of the volume of data found in the warehouse and the unpredictable nature of the processing that occurs against the data.

Eventually, the demands for information and analytics exceed what can be provided by the data warehouse. A new information construct is needed that can turn the integrated data provided by the data warehouse into information. This component of the corporate information factory is called the data mart and will be discussed in the next chapter.

4

The Data Mart Component

T he data warehouse is at the heart of information and analytical processing for the corporation, and its environment provides the basis for DSS processing. A data warehouse is often the first place integrated data is found in the corporation and is the appropriate place for historical data in the corporation.

The data warehouse, however, is not the answer to all the problems of DSS processing for the following reasons:

❏ As the data warehouse evolves, it becomes increasingly difficult to access because its design evolves to efficiently integrate and manage large volumes of quality data. This resulting design generally does not present the data in a legible format or in a fashion that optimizes query performance.

❏ The data warehouse is a truly corporate facility, so its data is not stored in an optimal fashion for any given department.

❏ The data warehouse is used by many people, so there is considerable competition to get to the resources required to get inside the data warehouse.

❑ The large volumes and organization of data in the data warehouse requires so much storage and processing power, that the cost of DSS computing facilities is very expensive.

For these reasons, individual DSS analysts are finding that as a data warehouse grows in size and maturity, they are attracted to another sort of DSS structure. This structure is called a data mart.

WHAT IS A DATA MART?

A data mart is a collection of data tailored to the DSS processing needs of a particular department. It is a subset of a data warehouse that has been customized to fit the needs of a department. Alternatively, a data mart can become a resource shared by multiple departments where common analytical needs exist (e.g., profitability analysis). Typically, data is summarized, resequenced, and merged as it passes from the data warehouse to the data mart. Usually, there are many data marts that attach to a data warehouse. Departments where data marts are often found include marketing, finance, accounting, engineering, and actuarial. Figure 4.1 depicts a data mart.

Data marts have some degree of kinship with a data warehouse, but they have their own distinctive characteristics as well. Figure 4.2 details some of the salient characteristics of a data mart.

A data mart is a subset of a data warehouse, containing a small amount of detailed data and a generous portion of summarized data. It contains a limited amount of history, significantly less history than might be found in the data warehouse. The data in the data mart is customized to address the needs of the department to which it belongs and DSS tool(s) selected for use.

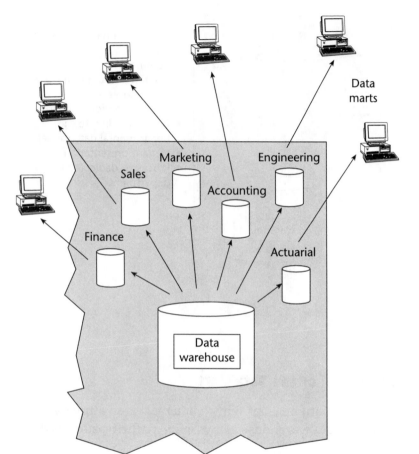

FIGURE 4.1
Data marts emanate from the data warehouse and feed the DSS needs of different departments.

There is only one legitimate feed into the data mart; that feed comes from the data warehouse. Unless there is some unusual circumstance, there is little or no exchange of data from one data mart to another. If there needs to be an exchange of data, the data to be exchanged is first passed to and stored at the data warehouse. Once housed at the data warehouse, the data is then passed to the data mart that would like to share the data. By following this discipline of exchange, reconcilability of data is maintained across the architecture.

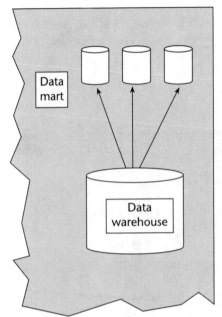

Data Marts
- A subset of data warehouse data
- Summarized
- Limited amount of history
- Very flexible
- Customized for a department
- Built according to the departmental data model
- Elegant presentation
- Processor dedicated to department

FIGURE 4.2
The data mart in the context of the corporate information factory.

The Appeal of the Data Mart

There are many reasons why a data mart is so attractive once the data warehouse grows in its maturity, such as the following:

❏ **Control.** A department can completely control the data and processing that occurs inside a data mart. When a department does its own processing from the data warehouse, the department must share resources and facilities with other departments that are also using the data warehouse. In some cases, the sharing of facilities can be very restrictive and uncomfortable.

❏ **Cost.** Because the department wants to analyze only a subset of the data found in the data warehouse, the cost of storage and processing is substantially less when the department moves the desired data off to a departmental machine. Because the departmental machine is significantly smaller than the machine that houses the data warehouse, it is less expensive—in terms of total cost and unit cost as well.

❏ **Customization.** As data passes into the data mart from the data warehouse, the data is customized to suit the peculiar needs of the department. The data that comes from the warehouse can:

❏ Have its keys restructured

❏ Be resequenced

❏ Be merged

❏ Be summarized

❏ Be edited, converted

In short, there are some powerful reasons why the data mart appears as an attractive augmentation to the data warehouse.

The appeal of data marts grows as the volume of the data in the data warehouse increases. As long as the data warehouse is small, the attraction of the data mart is not manifested. But as time passes, and the volume of the data and number of users grows, data marts become increasingly alluring.

The essence of a data mart is its flexibility and accessibility. Because there is much less data in a data mart than a data warehouse, the data mart is able to accommodate queries and requests of many sizes and varieties, at almost any time of day.

THE DATA WAREHOUSE TO THE DATA MART INTERFACE

One of the important components of the corporate information factory is the intranet connection between the data mart and the data warehouse.

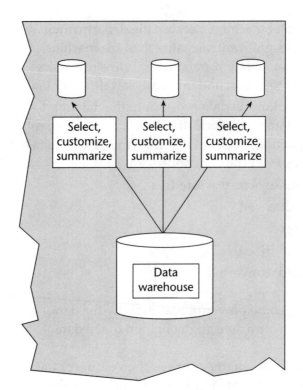

FIGURE 4.3

The interface between the data warehouse and the data marts is one where data warehouse data is selected, summarized, and customized. There is one interface for each department.

Figure 4.3 shows that as data is collected into the data mart from the data warehouse, it is selected, customized, and summarized. The flow of data is one that is unidirectional, from the data warehouse to the data mart. The flow occurs on an as-needed, requested basis, as demands are made to the data warehouse to flow data to the data mart. As a rule, the volume of data that flows over the interface is minimal, at least in comparison to the volumes of data that flow elsewhere in the CIF.

There is a separate flow and demand schedule for each department. There is almost never a consolidation of requirements for multiple departments for the coordination of the flow across the data warehouse to the data mart interface.

The programs that control the activity for the flow are normally created and maintained by the individual departments. It is only under very unusual circumstances that a DWA or a systems programmer would write the code that controls the flow of data into the data mart. The exception would be when a data mart was being created as a shared departmental resource.

DIFFERENT KINDS OF DATA MARTS

There are three popular kinds of data marts. The first represents a simple sample, subset or summary of the data warehouse. The other two support a style of analysis referred to as Online Analytical Processing (OLAP): MOLAP data marts and ROLAP data marts. Let's take a look at these two types of data marts in more detail.

MOLAP Data Marts

The first type of data mart is a Multidimensional Online Analytical Processing (MOLAP) data mart. It is one where the data is loaded into the data mart in a very structured manner and where *dimensions* of the data are created. Typical dimensions might be product, time, and location. There are usually a limited number—three or four—of dimensions for a MOLAP data mart.

Once the dimensions are created for the data mart, the data can be summarized along any number of dimensions. Once the summarizations have been created, the data can then be *drilled down,* from summarization to detail within the confines of the data mart.

The essence of a MOLAP data mart is a very high degree of flexibility and performance once the data has been loaded. (Ironically, in order to achieve a highly flexible structure, the data must be subjected to a highly inflexible amount of processing in order to prepare the data for entry into the multi-dimensional data mart.)

ROLAP Data Marts

The second kind of data mart is a Relational Online Analytical Processing (ROLAP) data mart. The processing is much more general in a ROLAP data mart than in a MOLAP data mart. The aim of ROLAP is to provide a multidimensional view of data using proven relational DBMS—two-dimensional—technology (Oracle, Informix, Sybase, etc.). In contrast, a MOLAP data mart facilitates this using specialized multidimensional DBMS technology. The amount of transformation and preparation of the data prior to entry into the ROLAP data mart is significantly less than the preparation required for entry into the MOLAP data mart environment.

It is of interest that many MOLAP data marts relate to the financial area because of the simplicity of business dimensions—few and stable—and demands for fast and predictable performance. In contrast, ROLAP data marts have become very popular in areas that are willing to trade-off predicable performance for the flexibility to manage and quickly alter large numbers of complex dimensions. ROLAP data marts are generally found in the areas of marketing, sales, and service.

A given department may have both a MOLAP and a set of ROLAP databases contained in the data mart. Indeed, there may be many different types of data mart databases within a department.

STAR JOIN SCHEMA AND DATA MARTS

The physical database design structure known as a star join schema has a particular affinity for the data mart in support of ROLAP (Figure 4.4). Star join schema organizes data so that it is easy to navigate and visualize. As a result, this database design technique greatly facilitates the simple and speedy access and analysis of data.

Star join schema is made up of fact tables and dimensions. The fact table represents the types of data that occur in great volume. The dimension tables represent smaller tables that are prejoined to the data in the fact table by means of a foreign key relationship. Because a star join schema entails physical denormalization, there is the implication that star join schemas are optimal for only one type and class of processing (i.e., a star join schema is not a structure that is useful for a general representation of data). Such an observation is true because star a join schema optimizes processing for one user or set of users and deoptimizes access of data for all other users.

This trade-off of optimization and deoptimization is indeed an accurate statement of facts. But because a data

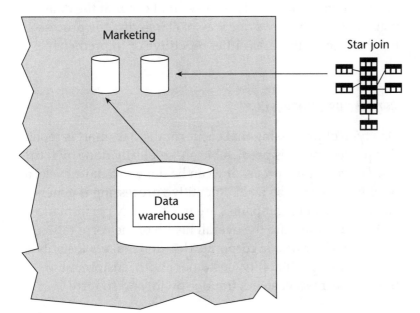

FIGURE 4.4

Star join schemas fit very nicely in the data mart environment.

mart is built for a department, a general pattern of access and analysis can be predicted for the department. The database designer is safe in specifying what the design of the star join schema will look like.

Note that such a proclamation cannot be made for data warehouses. Since there are so many different kinds of people using a data warehouse, it is almost impossible to say that there is a dominant pattern of usage for the data in the warehouse. That is why the star join schema is generally not a good fit for the data warehouse.

Such is not the case at all for a department. There is a much more homogeneous pattern of processing of data for a department, since there are fewer people, and the people have a similar interest and perspective in the execution of DSS processing.

PROCESSING AT THE DATA MART

There are many kinds of processes that occur at the data mart. Figure 4.5 shows one way of classifying the processing that occurs there, as either repetitive or unpredictable.

Repetitive Processing

One type of processing that occurs at the data mart is repetitive processing; it is predictable and typically done by farmers. The repetitive processing can be done in a daily cycle, a weekly cycle, and so forth. Repetitive processing is generally found where companies are tracking key performance metrics that measure the overall health of the corporation. These metrics provide corporate decision makers insights into product profitability, customer churn, customer lifetime value, market share, fraud growth, and so forth.

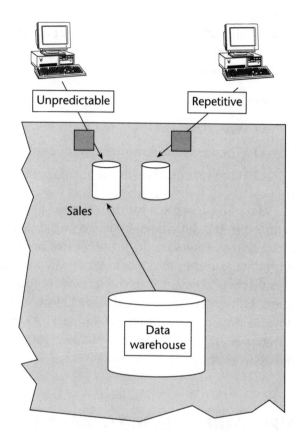

FIGURE 4.5
There are two basic kinds of processing found in the data mart environment: repetitive processes and unpredictable processes.

Unpredictable Processing

The second style of processing done at the data mart is unpredictable processing. This occurs when a farmer starts to become curious and to turn into an explorer. The unpredictable processing that occurs here can be of many varieties, from a simple addition of variables that have not been regularly added before to the selection and comparison of information over time that has never before been considered. Very often the unpredictable processing that occurs at the data mart leads to the need for drill-down processing, which occurs when a unit of summary data requires explanation. In drill-down processing, questions are asked, such as:

❑ What data went into this summarization?

❑ What data was excluded from this summarization?

❑ When was the summarization made?

❑ What formula was used in this summarization?

The simplest basis for drill-down starts with data that is found in the data mart, assuming a calculation has been made there. However, drill-down does not have to stop with data found in the data mart. It can continue by asking, What data was selected in the data warehouse for the data mart? How was the selection done? How was customization done as data passed into the data mart? At this point, drill-down processing has proceeded down into the data warehouse from the data mart.

FIRST ORDER, SECOND ORDER DATA

There are two types of data that are stored and managed in the data mart: first order data and second order data. Figure 4.6 shows the creation of first order and second order data in the data mart.

Data that is placed directly into the data mart from the data warehouse can be called first order data. But once placed into the data mart, the data can be further manipulated. Subsequent calculation and manipulation leads to data in the data mart that can be called second order data.

External data can legitimately flow directly into the data mart, as seen in Figure 4.7. When external data flows directly into the data mart, the implication is that the external data has no other use or application for any other data

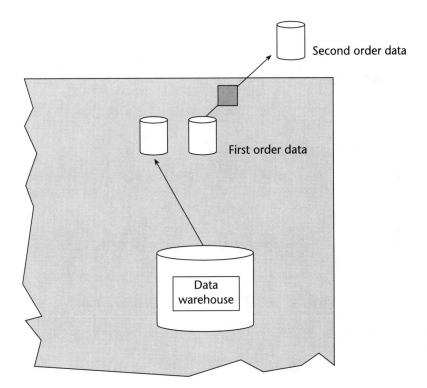

Second order data

First order data

Data warehouse

FIGURE 4.6
There are two types of data found in the data mart: first order data and second order data.

mart. If there is another use of the external data, it needs to first flow into the data warehouse, then flow from the data warehouse into the data mart.

METADATA

Another type of data found in the data mart is that of metadata. Data mart data does not have the rigid and formal metadata infrastructure that data warehouses have. Instead, metadata at the data mart comes in the flavor of metadata that is trapped and stored in the tools of access and analysis

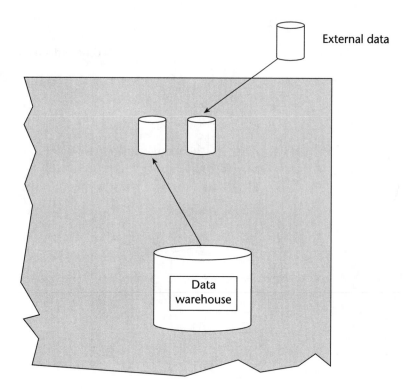

External data

Data warehouse

FIGURE 4.7
*External data can be loaded
into a data mart directly
when there is no other corporate use for the external data.*

that are found in the data mart. Figure 4.8 shows that metadata is an integral part—if informal—of the data mart environment.

Metadata can be a very important part of the data mart
environment. It can be useful to the farmer on those occasions when the farmer wishes to turn into an explorer.
However, metadata, at the data mart, must be a natural and
unconstraining part of the environment. The farmer at the
data mart needs to have a great deal of autonomy and does
not need a technology that limits what processing can and
cannot be done.

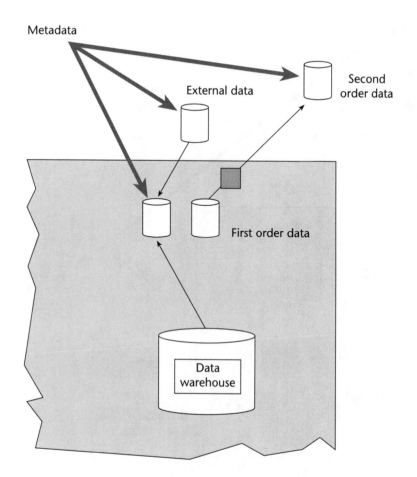

FIGURE 4.8
Metadata is a normal part of the data mart environment.

In some cases, it is desirable to have metadata control and management over more than one data mart. There can be a central data mart metadata controller that sits over more than one data mart, as suggested by Figure 4.9.

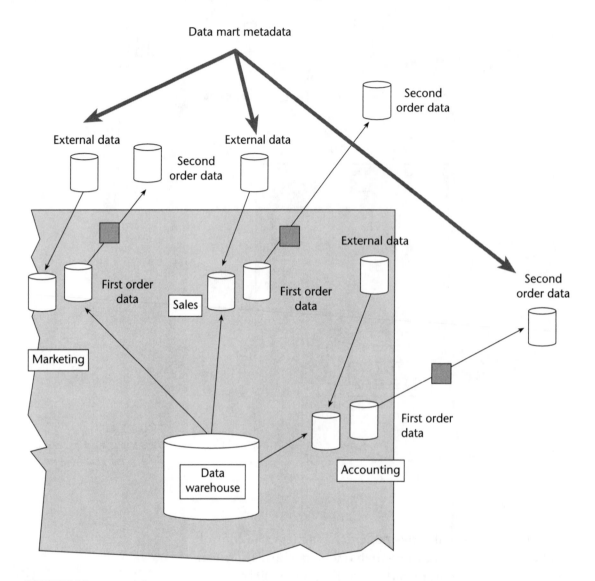

FIGURE 4.9

One possibility is for there to be a "super" metadata structure for more than one data mart.

SUMMARY

As data warehouses grow, another structure becomes attractive at the departmental level: a data mart. A data mart is a customized subset of data taken from the data warehouse; each department creates its own data mart.

In the final analysis, data marts provide business units the control and ability to interpret data warehouse data as needed to address their evolving business needs. In addition, data marts provide business units the autonomy to select and employ best-of-breed techniques and technology as their needs dictate. With this control and autonomy comes responsibility and accountability. Departments can no longer work independently. These business units must become active members of the corporate information community. They must be prepared to help define and enforce the use of data as a corporate resource.

There are three popular kinds of data marts—sample/summary, MOLAP, and ROLAP. Each these has its own unique characteristics.

Processing within the data mart can be classified as either repetitive or unpredictable against data that is primary or secondary. Metadata is seamlessly integrated into the DSS analyst environment and provides details necessary to understand, navigate, and use data mart data.

Now that we have talked about the components of the corporate information factory that integrate data—the data warehouse—and deliver information—the data mart—in support of strategic decision making, let's go to Chapter 5 and talk about the component of the architecture that helps makes these decisions actionable, the operational data store.

The Operational Data Store Component

For all of the benefits of a data warehouse and its associated data marts, there is still a need for collective, integrated operational, DSS/informational processing. When this need arises, an operational data store (ODS) is in order. An ODS is a hybrid structure that has equally strong elements of operational processing and DSS processing. This dual nature of the ODS easily makes it the most complex architectural structure in the corporate information factory (Figure 5.1).

WHAT IS AN OPERATIONAL DATA STORE?

An ODS is a collection of data containing detailed data for the purpose of satisfying the collective, integrated, operational needs of the corporation. Generally, these needs arise as strategic decisions are made using the data warehouse and data mart, and action is required. The ODS is:

Subject-oriented

Integrated

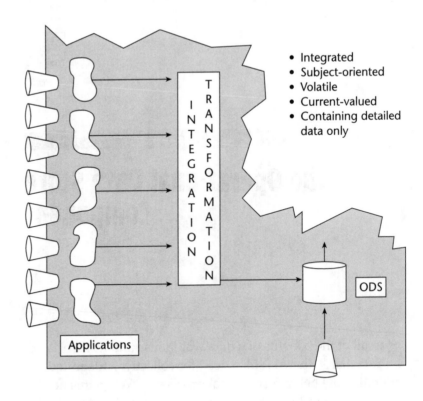

- Integrated
- Subject-oriented
- Volatile
- Current-valued
- Containing detailed data only

FIGURE 5.1
The operational data store.

Volatile

Current-valued

Detailed

The ODS looks very much like a data warehouse when it comes to its first two characteristics, subject orientation and integration. However, the remaining characteristics of an ODS are quite different from a data warehouse. Because of the very nature of these fundamental differences in types of data and processing, it is never acceptable to combine an ODS and a data warehouse into the same physical structure.

Volatility

An ODS is volatile. That means that an ODS can be updated as a normal part of processing. A data warehouse is non-volatile and is not updated under normal circumstances. Instead, a data warehouse contains snapshots; a new snapshot is created whenever a change needs to be reflected in the data warehouse.

Current-Valued

The second major difference is the timeliness of the data found in the ODS. An ODS typically contains daily, weekly, or maybe even monthly data, but the data ages very quickly in the ODS. The data warehouse, on the other hand, contains robust amounts of historical data. In fact, it may contain 5 or even 10 years worth of data.

Detailed

The third difference between an ODS and a data warehouse is that the ODS contains detailed data only, while a data warehouse contains both detailed and summary data. This characteristic is perhaps the most defining difference between a data warehouse and an ODS.

FEEDS INTO AND OUT OF THE OPERATIONAL DATA STORE

The ODS is simple; it has one primary feed into and one primary feed out of it (Figure 5.2).

The Integration and Transformation Layer Feed

The primary feed into the ODS is from the I & T layer. The feed out of the ODS is to the data warehouse. This ODS-to-data-warehouse feed is activated as data ages.

There is a secondary, rather small feed of data into the ODS, which is a feed directly from the external environment. While it is true that specialized applications

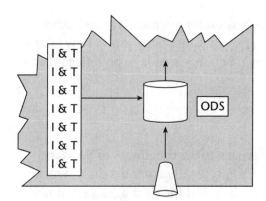

FIGURE 5.2
The feeds into and out of the ODS.

can be written that will allow data to go directly into the ODS, bypassing the I & T layer, these applications are fairly rare. Under normal circumstances, data enters the ODS by passing through the I & T layer.

DIFFERENT CLASSES OF THE OPERATIONAL DATA STORE

The I & T interface is of special interest because it governs the different types (or classes) of ODS. Consider the three different I & T interfaces shown in Figure 5.3:

- ❏ Class I: Asynchronous—one- to two-second delay
- ❏ Class II: Store and forward—two- to four-hour delay
- ❏ Class III: Batch processing—overnight

A single ODS will contain one, two, or perhaps all three classes of data.

Class I Operational Data Store

There is a synchronous interface where there is a very, very small amount of time that lapses between an applications

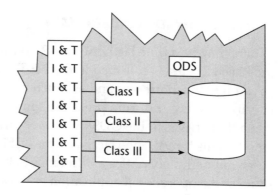

FIGURE 5.3
The three different classes of ODS are determined by the speed of the feed of data into the ODS.

transaction and the reflection of the transaction in the ODS. The amount of time is typically one second or less. This type of interface is called a Class I ODS. In this class, there is very little serious work that can be done to the data as it passes through the I & T layer because there simply isn't time to do very much. The transaction passes through to the ODS in a fairly complete manner. For all practical purposes, the end user never sees that there is a time lag between an operational transaction execution and the reflection of that transaction in the ODS when the ODS is Class I.

Class II Operational Data Store

There may be a matter of an hour or two from the time a transaction is created and interacted in the application environment until that transaction is reflected in the ODS. This type of ODS is called a Class II ODS. The I & T layer holds the data in abeyance in a store-and-forward mode. Because of the time lag, a serious amount of work can be done to the transaction data as it passes through the I & T layer. The data shows up as truly integrated data in the ODS. The end user can notice a difference between the data in the operational applications and the ODS while the data is held in a store-and-forward mode.

Class III Operational Data Store

There may be a time lag between 12 hours and a day as transaction data is collected in the I & T interface. This is an overnight batch process and as much integration of data as desired can occur during processing in the I & T layer. The data that arrives at the ODS can be very integrated in this mode. This type of interface is a Class III interface. The end user can definitely notice a difference between the values of data in the operational application environment and the ODS as the data sits in the I & T layer awaiting processing.

Determining the Class

There are many technological implications to the intranet technology that must be considered here, such as:

- ❏ Speed of movement of data into the ODS
- ❏ Volume of data that must be moved
- ❏ Volume of data that must be stored in intermediate locations during I & T processing
- ❏ Update of data and integrity of transaction processing

The choice of whether a Class I, II, or III ODS will be created is the first and one of the most important decisions the systems architect must make. Figure 5.4 outlines some of the considerations involved in the choice of a Class I, II, or III ODS.

Furthermore, if integration is a primary consideration, then a Class I ODS is not a very good choice because not very much integration can be achieved with it. For these reasons then, there must be a very serious business justification for a Class I ODS. As a rule, a Class II or a Class III ODS serves most organizations' needs for most processing.

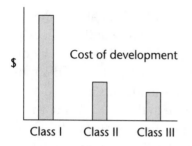

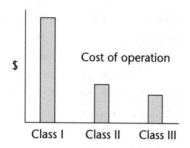

FIGURE 5.4
The cost of development and operation for a Class I ODS is significantly higher than the corresponding costs for a Class II and a Class III ODS.

DYNAMIC SUMMARY DATA

One of the distinguishing characteristics of an ODS is the fact that it only stores detailed data. Certainly, summary data can be created from detailed data, but storing that summary data once it is created is an entirely different matter. The summary data that is created in the ODS can be called dynamic summary data. This is data whose accuracy of summarization depends upon the moment of calculation.

Figure 5.5 shows a calculation that is made for a bank's current collective balance for IBM Corporation. At 10:37 A.M.,

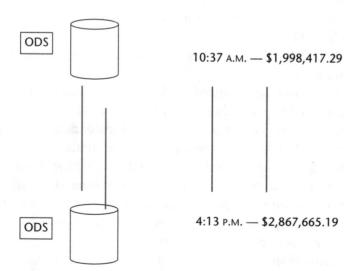

10:37 A.M. — $1,998,417.29

4:13 P.M. — $2,867,665.19

FIGURE 5.5
Dynamic summary data: The accuracy of the calculation depends on the moment in time that the calculation is made.

IBM has a collective balance of $1,998,417.29. Later in the day, at 4:13 P.M., another calculation is made of the collective balance of IBM, showing $2,867,665.19. The accuracy of the summary data found in the ODS is a function of the moment in time when the calculation is made. It would be a mistake to store the 10:37 A.M. value in the ODS because it would be tempting to use that value for a business decision at 4:13 P.M. The business decision at 4:13 P.M. may well be a very different business decision than the one made at the earlier time. For this reason, dynamic summary data is not normally stored in an ODS.

STATIC SUMMARY DATA

Now consider the summary data found in a data warehouse. Suppose that on Monday, a manager asks an analyst to determine what expenses were for the last quarter in a department. The analyst calculates that quarterly expenses were $101,768.19 for the department.

Now suppose that another manager asks an analyst to make the same calculation on Friday. The analyst should calculate exactly the same amount—$101,768.19. There should be no variation in the amount calculated, even though the calculation is made at a different moment in time.

This type of summary data is called static summary data and is perfectly safe to place in a data warehouse. In fact, it is wasteful not to place this type of data in a warehouse. In the data warehouse, the DSS analyst is less interested in what expenses look like this instant and more interested in how expenses trend over time, compared to forecast, and compared to last year. In addition, the DSS analyst expects these complex questions to be answered in a very short time (2-3 minutes). This can only be accomplished through liberal use of static summaries in the data warehousing environment. Because of the differences between dynamic summary data and static summary data, summary data should not be stored in an ODS, but in a data warehouse and/or data mart.

THE OPERATIONAL DATA STORE WORKLOAD

The ODS environment is the most technologically challenging environment because there are elements of very different kinds of processing that must constructively cohabitate in the same technological infrastructure (Figure 5.6).

Loading the Data

One kind of processing that must be done in the ODS is that of loading data. In the case of a Class I ODS, the loading is done in an online manner. The challenges faced in this environment are generally associated with the sophistication of technology or the lack of key technologies in the application and/or legacy environments.

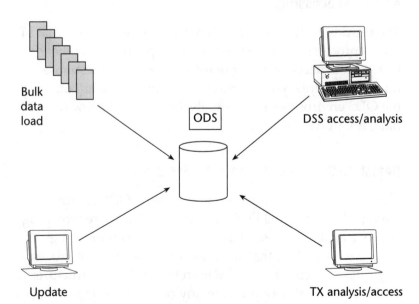

Bulk data load

ODS

DSS access/analysis

Update

TX analysis/access

FIGURE 5.6
The kinds of processing that occur in the ODS environment.

In the case of a Class II or III ODS, loading is done asynchronously. The challenges surface when loading large volumes of data. This generally results in load processes that are complex to develop, certify, and maintain.

Update Processing

The second kind of processing that can be done in the ODS environment (Class I, II, or III) is that of update processing. Even though direct update is not frequently done, it still must be accommodated. When direct update must be accomplished, there is a technological implication of integrity of update. This is achieved within the confines of the DBMS structure by means of facilities that COMMIT work to be applied to the database, ROLLBACK work that has not been COMMITed and RECOVER work that has been COMMITed and lost. Even though update may be done for only a small number of transactions, *all* active transactions in the system pay the price of overhead for update.

Access Processing

The third type of processing that occurs in the ODS is that of access processing. There may be many people using the ODS that expect consistent two-to-three-second response time. In fact, this type of processing is the dominant one in the ODS environment and entails the access of a few rows of data, not update of data.

Decision-Support Systems Analysis

The fourth type of processing found in the ODS environment is the occasional DSS analysis of data, where sweeping analysis is made across many records. The complicating aspect of the ODS is that *all* of the different styles of processing must be accommodated within the ODS infrastructure. The problem is that optimizing any one style of processing compromises all other styles of processing. Said differently, when the designer of the ODS optimizes any one style of processing, the designer does so at the expense of all other styles of processing. The best the designer can do is achieve a comfortable level of performance for all styles of processing in the ODS. It is because of this compromise that the ODS is the most complicated of all the architectural constructs within the corporate information factory.

DIFFERENT PROCESSING WINDOWS

In order to achieve the compromise between the types of processing, the ODS designer must carefully divide the ODS day into different processing windows, as shown in Figure 5.7. One of the most important reasons why the ODS processing window must be divided into a series of *mini* processing windows is that in order to achieve consistent processing time, that workload must be *homogeneous*.

What Is a homogeneous Workload?

A homogeneous workload is one where the different types of processing that reside in the workload are not mixed.

8:00 A.M. →	12:00 noon	→ 1:00 P.M. →	5:00 P.M. →	7:00 P.M. →	12:00 midnight	→ 5:00 A.M. →	8:00 A.M.
Access tx processing/ tx update processing	Bulk load access tx processing	Access tx processing/t x update processing	DSS access/ analysis	DSS access/ analysis/bulk load	Bulk load/ image copy/ data monitor/ utilities	DSS access/ analysis/free time	

FIGURE 5.7
The cycle of daily processing for the ODS environment.

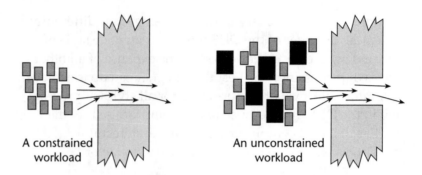

FIGURE 5.8
In order to achieve consistent and good response time, the workload flowing through the system needs to be constrained.

A constrained workload

An unconstrained workload

Figure 5.8 shows the difference between a homogeneous workload and a heterogeneous workload in terms of system throughput.

On the lefthand side of Figure 5.8 is a homogeneous workload where only transactions of a given type—small, fast-running transactions—are found. In the environment on the left, flow through the system bottlenecks is unimpeded and there is an efficient and quick flow. Such a system exhibits good response time.

Now consider the workload represented on the right side of Figure 5.8. In this workload there is a mixture of different kinds of transactions—very small, fast-running transactions and large, slow-running transactions. The practice of keeping workloads homogeneous is called adherence to the *standard work unit* and has been known and practiced by online system designers for years. The concepts of the standard work unit apply to the ODS every bit as much as they have applied to OLTP.

EXTERNAL DATA IN THE OPERATIONAL DATA STORE

External data can be placed in the ODS just as it is placed in other parts of the corporate information factory. Metadata is likewise a part of the ODS environment. While metadata is useful in the ODS environment, it is not nearly as important as it is in the data warehouse or the data mart environment.

SUMMARY

The ODS is a hybrid architectural construct containing some elements of data warehousing and some application characteristics. It operates on a mixed workload and is easily the most difficult component of the CIF to construct and operate.

An ODS is not an essential part of the CIF. Some companies operate quite nicely with no ODS. Other companies find an ODS to be indispensable when their existing applications environment do not provide the necessary integration to support evolving business management activities resulting from business intelligence gained using the data warehouse. This is commonplace in many marketing, sales, and service organizations. These organizations generally use the data warehouse to formulate strategies on how to best treat their customers and use the ODS to support contact activities related to execution of these strategies.

The feed into the ODS is the I & T layer. In addition, occasionally data is entered directly into the ODS.

There are three types of ODS: Class I, Class II, and Class III. The class of an ODS depends on the speed with which data is passed from the I & T layer. As a single ODS matures, it is possible that it may contain all classes of data.

The ODS contains dynamic summary data, data whose accuracy depends on the moment of calculation. Because of the ever-changing nature of dynamic summary data, it is normally not stored in the ODS.

The ODS operates on a severely mixed workload. Because of the dramatic differences in the nature of the workload, the ODS day is divided into slices. There is the OLTP time slice, the batch time slice, and the DSS time slice.

We have discussed the component of the corporate information factory responsible for the organization and management of data. In Chapter 6, we will review the component of the corporate information factory responsible for the capture, translation, and movement of data: the integration and transformation (I & T) layer.

6

The Integration and Transformation Layer Component

T he source of data for the ODS and the data warehouse is
an architectural component known as the integration and
transformation layer (the I & T layer), discussed briefly in
Chapter 5. Unlike the ODS, data warehouse, and data marts
which are made up primarily of data, the I & T layer is
made up primarily of programs. In the spirit of the
metaphor of an actual factory, the I & T layer is where most
of the work of the factory takes place. Figure 6.1 shows the I
& T layer (or interface).

WHAT IS THE INTEGRATION AND TRANSFORMATION LAYER?

The I & T interface is the place where unintegrated data
from the applications environment is combined—or integrated—and transformed into corporate data. As we will
see later in this chapter, significant transformations take

FIGURE 6.1

*The I & T layer: A group of
programs dedicated to the
capture, transformation, and
movement of data from the
applications environment to
the ODS and the data warehouse environment.*

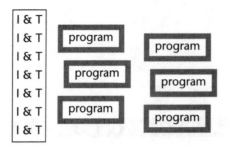

place as data moves through the I & T layer. Once this data
has been molded into a corporate asset, the I & T layer loads
it into the data warehouse and/or ODS for access by the
end-user community.

An Unstable Interface

The I & T interface is a very unstable set of programs, since
they constantly change over time for the following reasons
(Figure 6.2):

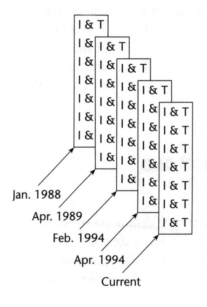

The I & T layer is constantly
changing over time.

The first iteration of the I & T layer
is the most unstable.

First to second iteration—major
changes

Second to third iteration—changes

Third to fourth iteration—minor
changes

. . . .

nth to n+1th iteration—tweaks

FIGURE 6.2

*The I & T layer is constantly
changing.*

❏ **The applications environment is constantly changing.** Every time the applications environment changes, one or more programs in the I & T interface must also change.

❏ **The data warehouse is built incrementally.** Pieces of the data warehouse are added over time; with each new increment comes changes to the I & T layer.

❏ **The data warehouse is built iteratively.** In many cases, after the DSS analyst has seen what arrives in the data warehouse, the DSS analyst calls for a re-shaping and retooling of the environment.

Complexity of processing is not the only factor shaping the I & T layer. On occasion, the speed with which data can be moved through the I & T layer is a consideration as well, as illustrated in Figure 6.3.

As an example of a case where speed of movement of data through the I & T layer becomes a factor, consider the processing of data for a Class I ODS. In the case of a Class I ODS, the amount of time that data spends in the I & T layer is less than a second. When data is moved through the I & T layer at that speed, very little complex or significant pro-

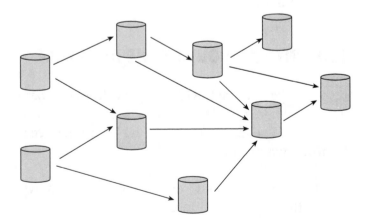

FIGURE 6.3
The speed of movement throughout the I & T layer is normally not an issue, with the exception of movement to Class I ODS.

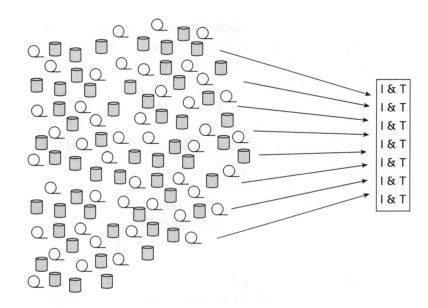

FIGURE 6.4

The primary issue of I & T processing is that of processing huge volumes of data.

cessing can be done. In essence, transaction information passes through the I & T layer untouched in order to optimize on the speed of processing.

Complexity of processing and speed of processing, however, are not the only things that can be an issue. Another issue is that of the volume of data that needs to pass through the I & T layer. Figure 6.4 shows that large volumes of data can frequently back up at the application awaiting processing in the I & T layer.

FEEDS INTO AND OUT OF THE INTERFACE

The primary feed into the I & T layer is from the many applications where raw detailed data is captured and audited (Figure 6.5). The feed of data into the I & T interface is complex from two perspectives:

   1. There is a massive amount of data that moves through the interface.

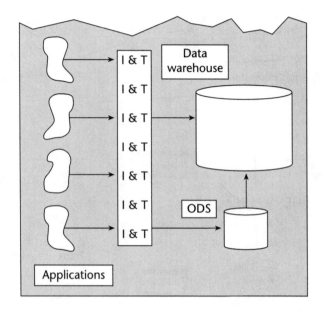

FIGURE 6.5
The feeds into and out of the I & T layer.

2. The amount of work that is done to the data is non-trivial.

The feeds out of the I & T layer go to two places:

❏ Into the ODS
❏ Into the data warehouse

THE COMPLEX INTEGRATION AND TRANSFORMATION INTERFACE

The I & T interface is comprised of many different programs that accomplish many different functions. Figure 6.6 shows how complex the I & T interface can be.

I & T programs can do one of the following functions:

❏ Merely read data from one database and pass data to another program.

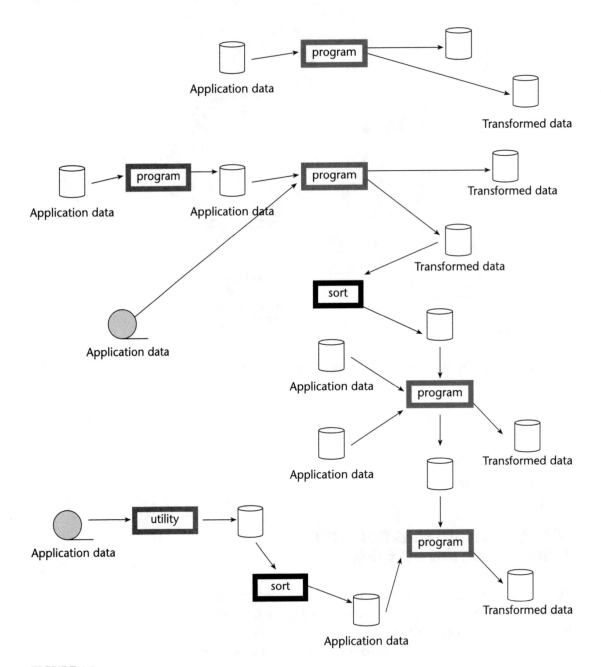

FIGURE 6.6
What the I & T environment looks like from a visceral perspective.

Data model

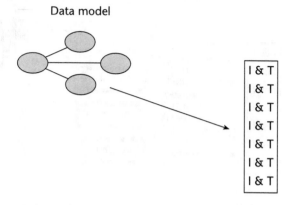

FIGURE 6.7
The I & T layer is heavily influenced by the data model.

❑ Do transformations that standardize data using a common set of encoding, derivation, formatting, and substitution rules.

❑ Map the transformed data to the correct location in the data warehouse and/or ODS.

❑ Produce intermediary files that are then used as input into other programs.

❑ Finally, if there is more than one input source, they can produce more than one file as output.

Data is then resequenced, as input comes from external data and reference files as well. In short, a tremendous amount of work is done to the data that has been originally gathered by the applications to recast that data into the form of integrated data.

The overall plan for integration is provided by the data model that sits atop the I & T layer. Figure 6.7 shows the relationship between the data model and the I & T layer.

THE ROLE OF THE DATA MODEL

The logical data model acts like a blueprint that describes how data should look in the corporate information factory.

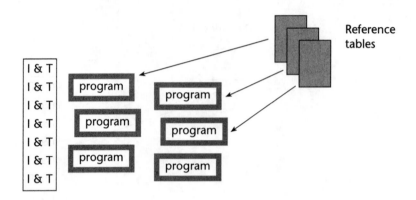

FIGURE 6.8

Reference tables are a standard part of the I & T layer.

From these specifications, the *builder* creates I & T programs that transform raw materials provided by the applications environment into the foundation, frame, roof, siding, and interior that make up the CIF. The logical data model intellectually unifies the work that is done by the many programs that go into the I & T layer.

More than just raw detailed input goes into the I & T layer. Reference data and external data, can all be input into the I & T layer, as seen by Figure 6.8.

CREATING METADATA

One of the important outputs of the I & T activities is that of metadata that describes the process of transformation, as illustrated by Figure 6.9.

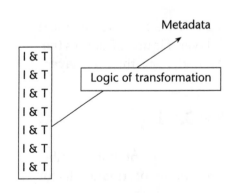

FIGURE 6.9

The logic of transformation is put into the metadata environment. It is one of the most important products of the I & T layer.

The metadata that is output in Figure 6.9 is descriptive of the logic of transformation. At the end of the day, the DSS analyst using the corporate information factory needs to know exactly what transpired in the logic that was executed in the I & T layer. The logic of processing is captured in the metadata that describes what is occurring in the I & T layer. The information that is captured is technically not *metadata* but *metaprocess* information.

PROCESSING IN THE INTEGRATION AND TRANSFORMATION INTERFACE

The kind of processing that occurs in the I & T interface is varied and complex. Perhaps the most basic kind of processing is that of key transformation. Figure 6.10 depicts some of the considerations of key transformation.

There are three applications that have a different key structure for a customer. Application A has its unique key structure, application B has its own key structure, and application C uses a social security number for its key. In order to achieve uniformity of key structure, the DWA has several choices:

❏ Convert the key for all applications to social security number

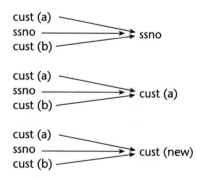

FIGURE 6.10

Three possibilities for resolving inconsistent key structures.

❑ Convert applications B and C to the key structure suggested by A

❑ Convert all applications to a new key structure

Exactly which strategy for key conversion is proper is a function of several factors including:

❑ What does the data model specify?

❑ Is there a dominant application?

❑ Is most of the data already in a standard key format?

Adding an element of time to an operational key structure is a common thing to do as data passes through the I & T layer (Figure 6.11).

An element of time consists of some form or measurement of time, such as a day, a week, or a month.

In many cases, data in the applications environment will not include time as part of the key structure. In order to fit in the data warehouse, an element of time needs to be added, usually to the tail end of the key structure. Some key structures naturally have time included, such as transaction data. Other key structures do not have time as part of the key. The creation of profile records is a very common activity as data passes from the applications environment to the data warehouse or the ODS environment.

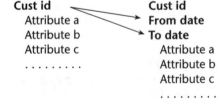

FIGURE 6.11
The addition of an element of time.

Who Is in Charge of Integration and Transformation Processing

I & T processing is in the domain of the DWA who understands the technical and business ramifications of running it. To let any other organizational function build and manage the I & T interface is a mistake. They generally do not understand these ramifications and are focused and measured on their ability to keep the applications, thus the wheels of the corporation, running. This leaves little time to understand or support the I & T layer.

Profile Record or Aggregate Records

The Profile records are very useful for changing the granularity of data and managing the volume of data that ends up in the data warehouse (Figure 6.12). Tremendous condensation of data is possible with their creation. Profile records are created from many small units of detail residing in the application environment that are combined into a single aggregate record.

Encoding Structures

Standardization of encoding structures is a very common activity in the I & T interface, as seen by Figure 6.13. In this figure, different applications have represented gender in different manners. Logic in the I & T interface is required to

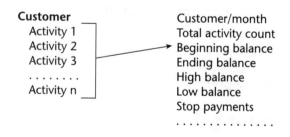

FIGURE 6.12

Creating profile or aggregate records from the many occurrences at the applications environment.

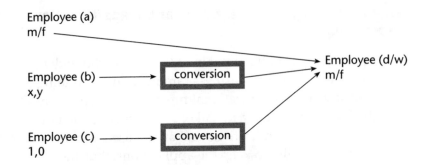

FIGURE 6.13

Conversion of encoded values to achieve consistency is another transformation activity.

create a standard representation of encoded data in the data warehouse and the ODS environment.

Simple Reformatting

Simple reformatting of dates and other fields is a common activity in the I & T interface. Figure 6.14 shows a simple reformatting of dates, where a date field has been restructured to accommodate the year 2000.

Mathematical Conversion

Mathematical conversion is another common I & T activity. Figure 6.15 illustrates an example of a simple mathematical conversion.

There may be many reasons for a mathematical conversion, such as:

❑ A change in accounting periods

❑ A conversion of monetary rates

❑ Account adjustments

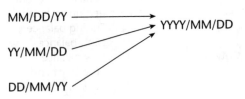

FIGURE 6.14

Reformatting data to achieve consistency.

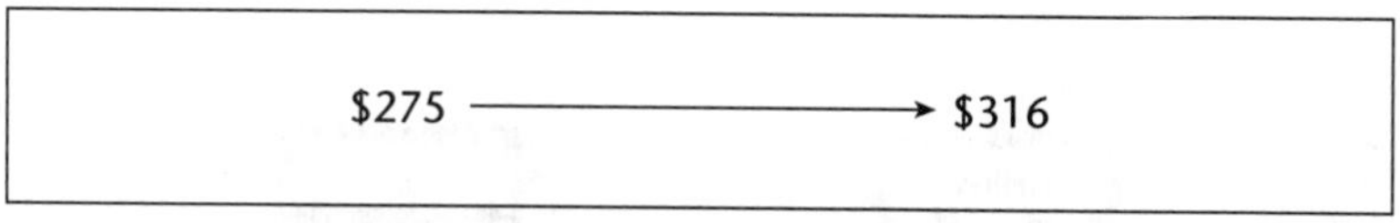

$275 \longrightarrow $316

FIGURE 6.15
Mathematical conversion.

MULTIPLE SOURCES OF DATA

On occasions the DWA will have more than one source of data to choose from when moving data from applications into the data warehouse or ODS. On those occasions, the DWA must specify logic that determines the best source of data and under what conditions it is to be chosen (Figure 6.16).

Resequencing Data

Resequencing data as it passes through the I & T interface is another activity, as seen in Figure 6.17. Resequencing data is a simple thing to do. The only complicating factor is that of managing the volumes of data that must be resequenced.

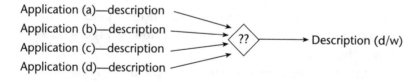

Application (a)—description
Application (b)—description
Application (c)—description
Application (d)—description

?? → Description (d/w)

FIGURE 6.16
Choosing the best data from multiple sources.

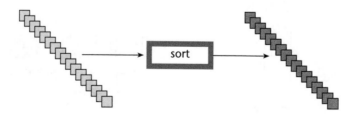

sort

FIGURE 6.17
Resequencing data.

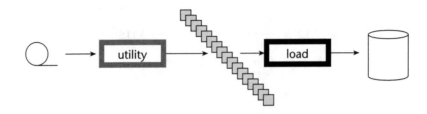

FIGURE 6.18
Using log tapes as a source for refreshment.

LOG TAPES AS A SOURCE FOR REFRESHMENT

Occasionally it makes sense to use log and journal tapes that have been created as a by product of application transaction processing as input into the I & T interface. Log and journal tapes can be a very efficient way of gathering data that needs to be transacted into the data warehouse. Figure 6.18 shows this option.

When log and journal tapes are used, the data is read by means of a utility in order to capture it off the log tape. Once captured, the data is ready to be entered into the standard processing that occurs in the I & T interface.

CHANGING PLATFORMS

In many cases, data resides on one architectural platform in the applications environment and on another platform in the data warehouse or the ODS environment. Figure 6.19 shows this change to data.

Many changes must occur when the underlying hardware platform changes which must be effected in the I & T

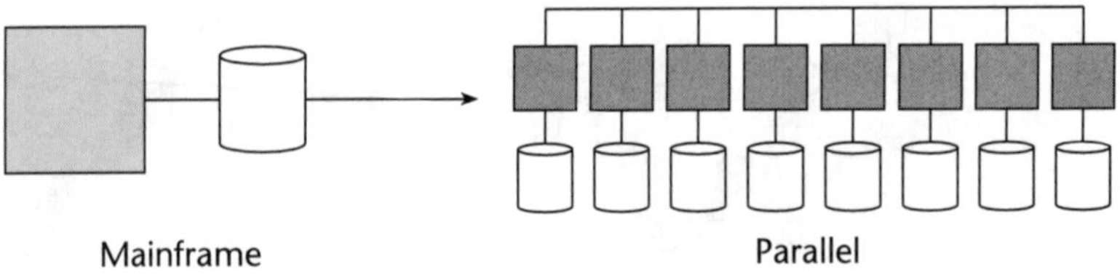

FIGURE 6.19
Switching hardware architectures is a common transformation.

Mainframe   Parallel

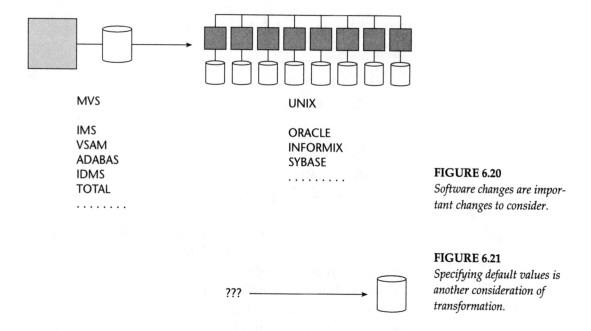

MVS

IMS
VSAM
ADABAS
IDMS
TOTAL
. . . .

UNIX

ORACLE
INFORMIX
SYBASE
. . . .

FIGURE 6.20
Software changes are important changes to consider.

FIGURE 6.21
Specifying default values is another consideration of transformation.

interface. However, changes in the hardware platform are not the only fundamental changes that must occur. Software changes in platforms are an important consideration as well, as seen in Figure 6.20.

DEFAULT VALUES

Sometimes there will be data elements processed by the I & T layer that are not populated. On these occasions the DWA needs to have specified default values, as seen in Figure 6.21.

SUMMARY

The I & T layer is made up of programs that pass data from the applications environment to the ODS or the data warehouse environment. As the data is passed, it is integrated through a complex process. The integration process includes activities, such as:

❑ Key resolution
❑ Resequencing of data
❑ Restructuring of data layouts
❑ Merging of data
❑ Aggregation of data
❑ Summarization of data

The I & T layer's structure is heavily influenced by the data model, which serves as the intellectual road map for the work that is accomplished by the I & T programs. Reference tables are a standard part of the I & T interface.

One of the important outputs from the I & T layer is the logic of transformation which is placed in the metadata repository. The metadata that represents the logic of transformation is captured and stored over time; this process of maintaining metadata occurences is referred to as *versioning*.

Occasionally, the speed of processing through the I & T programs becomes an issue. In the case of a Class I ODS, speed of processing becomes an issue, since the I & T interface processes huge volumes of data.

So far, we have talked about where the data is stored for strategic analysis—the data warehouse and data mart. We have talked about where operational integration is performed to support actions resulting from strategic analysis—the operational data store. We have talked about where the data is captured, transformed, and loaded into storage—the integration and transformation layer. In the next chapter, we will review the primary source of raw material for the corporate information factory—the applications.

CHAPTER SEVEN

Applications Component

Applications have been in existence since the earliest systems were built. The development life cycle for applications, the day-to-day operation of the applications, and the ongoing maintenance that applications require is well documented. For all of these reasons, applications are well known to almost anyone looking at the corporate information factory.

Another way to think of the applications in the CIF is as a collection vehicle for raw detailed data that is responsible for:

❏ Gathering detailed data
❏ Interacting directly with the end user
❏ Auditing and adjusting data
❏ Editing data

Undoubtedly, the applications in the corporate information factory accomplish more than the simple functions listed here. For example, applications collect this data as part of their core function to automate key business processes within the corporation, such as accounts payable, accounts receivable, order processing, and transaction processing. The simple functions, however, are found in one form or another throughout the applications environment.

DATED APPLICATIONS

The applications specified 20 years ago to address business problems are no longer sufficient alone to address the evolving needs of business. The corporation's business climate has changed dramatically over time, but the application infrastructure representing the business of the corporation has not. Therefore, applications are not without their own unique challenges.

If applications were easy to change once built, there would be no problem. However, applications are notoriously difficult to change once implemented, because over time, they have become a collective millstone around the neck of the corporation; each new application merely adds weight to it. In this sense, applications are anything but easy to understand and manage.

The inability to be responsive to change is not the only challenge associated with applications. Another characteristic of applications which challenges the DWA is their unintegrated nature.

UNINTEGRATED APPLICATIONS

The applications are unintegrated for a variety of reasons:

❑ The applications were built to suit the needs of one group, then another.
❑ Applications were acquired as part of a corporate merger.

❏ Applications were first built in-house, then augmented by third-party software packages.

❏ The cost justification process applied to development of applications did not allow for anything other than an immediate and obvious set of requirements to be addressed, thereby limiting the extensibility and reuse of the application solution.

This lack of integration of applications surfaces in many ways, such as:

❏ Inconsistent key structures

❏ Inconsistent encoding structures

❏ Inconsistent structuring of data

❏ Inconsistent reference structures of data

❏ Inconsistent definitions of data

❏ Inconsistent code and calculations

❏ Inconsistent reporting

The lack of integration across the application environment severely affects its credibility and agility.

APPLICATIONS RESPONSE TIME

One of the features of the applications environment is the level (i.e., the speed) of responsiveness to the users of its systems. Users of applications often expect very good response time for the transactions that are being executed by the application. Good response time usually means a response in two to three seconds from the moment the request was issued.

It is reasonable that the end user expect very good transaction response time because:

❏ Very little data is involved in any given transaction

❏ Transactions are run on technology capable of giving good response time

❏ The transactions operation details data that are directly and personally relevant to the consumer

In some cases, the consumer interacts directly with the system, such as through an ATM. In other cases, the consumer interacts with the systems through an intermediary, such as an airline service professional or a bank teller.

MIGRATING FROM AN UNINTEGRATED STATE

Because the lack of integration of applications is a very large problem, it is normal for an organization to migrate from an unintegrated state to an integrated state.

The problem with the migration suggested in Figure 7.1 is that it is expensive, painful, and slow to accomplish. Older unintegrated applications, for all of their faults, are very difficult to fundamentally alter largely because they run the day-to-day business. One of the burning issues of applications is how to achieve this migration. There are five key steps that are fairly common to the reengineering of these applications:

1. Define the strategic business vision. This includes a conceptual description of the evolving business landscape, and the imperatives and competencies needed to compete on this landscape.

2. Define the information architecture needed to support the strategic business vision.

3. Assess the current application inventory and how this inventory aligns to the competencies defined in the strategic business vision.

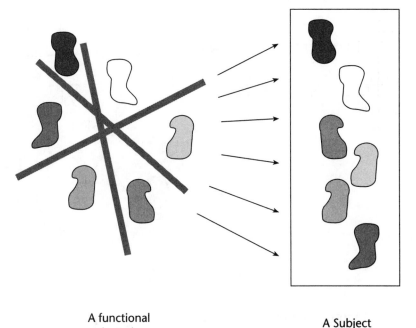

A functional
orientation

A Subject
orientation

FIGURE 7.1
*The transformation from an
unintegrated state to an
integrated state is slow,
expensive, and still at a
detailed level.*

4. Develop a migration plan that defines and priori-
   tizes a series of three-to-four month projects that
   will evolve, retire, or develop new applications to
   support the business vision. Each of these strategic
   projects should deliver immediate and incremental
   value to the business.

5. Execute the migration plan. To expedite the migration plan, companies may elect to purchase third-
   party application solutions from such companies as
   SAP, PeopleSoft, and Oracle.

EXTERNAL DATA/METADATA AND APPLICATIONS

Like other parts of the CIF, applications make use of external data and metadata. Figure 7.2 shows this relationship.

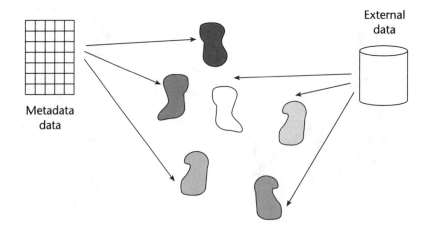

Metadata
data

FIGURE 7.2
*External data and metadata
data are made available to the
applications.*

External data plays an important role in supporting
detailed requests, at the most granular level. Applications
also make use of metadata. Metadata keeps track of where
data is coming from (end user, external companies, etc.),
how data is being used (billing, order processing, etc.), and
where data is going (data warehouse, ODS, etc.). Probably
the most interesting distinction between metadata for the
applications versus metadata for the data warehouse or
ODS is that it is more important to the systems developer
than it is to the end user. The systems developer is responsible for changes to the applications which interpret the data
and, therefore, needs the knowledge of the applications provided by the metadata. Generally speaking, the end user
deals with the applications environment through the system
developer. In some respects, the systems developer becomes
the "living" metadata repository for the end-user community. This is in contrast to the data warehouse where the end
user is directly involved in evolving the DSS capabilities
which interpret the data and, thus, needs access to the metadata that describes it.

FEEDS INTO AND OUT OF THE APPLICATIONS ENVIRONMENT

The flow of data into and out of the applications is simple. Figure 7.3 shows that raw detailed data is collected directly from the end user. This data represents the input feed of data into the CIF. The raw detailed data then flows out of the applications to the I & T interface.

An important architectural component of the applications environment is a component known as the system of record. This resulting source of data is captured by the I & T layer, transformed and loaded into the data warehouse and/or ODS. The system of record represents the best source of data because it is:

❏ The most complete source

❏ The most accurate source

❏ The most current source

❏ The source that most closely conforms to the corporate data model

Note that the data in the system of record does not have to be perfect and may occasionally contain imperfections. Also, note that the system of record may contain multiple sources for the same unit of data. Under one set of conditions the system of record may reside in Application

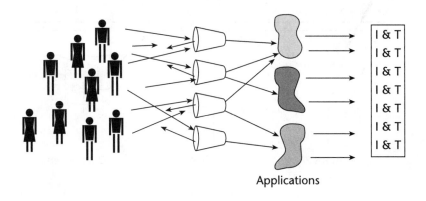

Applications

FIGURE 7.3
Applications feed data into the I & T layer.

A. Under a different set of conditions, the system of record may reside in Application B, and so forth.

A good way to understand the relationship of data and processing in applications versus data and processing in the ODS and the data warehouse is to think of data as operating on a continuum of time. This continuum is suggested by the measurement of seismic activity. In Figure 7.4, a stylus is constantly measuring seismic activity and tape is constantly moving beneath the stylus. Applications represent the recording of the seismic activity and the first few seconds after the recording has been made. The ODS captures the next few seconds in the life of the data. Then the data warehouse captures the data historically.

The continuous spectrum of the flow of data and how the data resides in different components of the CIF explains the relationship of the data in the corporate information factory to the architectural component.

FIGURE 7.4

One way of viewing the relationship of the age of data within the corporate information factory: Imagine a seismograph tracking the shaking of the earth. The data that is gathered has a different age. Based on the age of the data, there is a different use of the data and different implications to the organization.

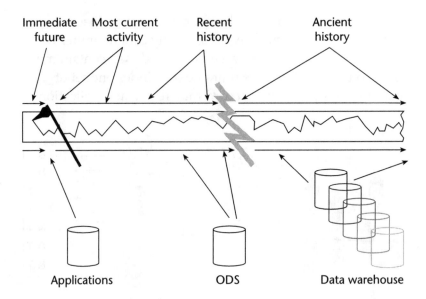

SUMMARY

Applications are the component of the data warehouse where data is gathered directly, either from the end user or directly from the consumer. The history of applications are such that they are unintegrated. This lack of integration shows up in many places, such as:

❑ Key structure of data
❑ Definition of the data
❑ Data layout
❑ Encoding structure of the data
❑ The usage of reference tables

Transaction response time is an important issue for the applications component of the CIF. Another important issue is the integration of the applications. Unfortunately, applications are difficult and slow to integrate once they have been built and installed.

Data leaves the application layer and is fed into the I & T layer. An important decision to be made by the I & T layer is in selecting the system of record, the source of data that will flow into the I & T layer. The system of record represents the best data, not necessarily perfect data, that the corporation has collected in the applications.

Congratulations! You now understand the key components of the corporate information factory responsible for:

❑ Capturing corporate data—the applications
❑ Integrating and transforming this data—the I & T layer
❑ Using this data—the data warehouse, data marts, operational data store, and people

Now, it is time to discuss the communication fabric that physically binds these components—the Internet and intranet.

8

The Internet and Intranet Components

The components of the corporate information factory—data marts, the data warehouse, the ODS, the I & T layer, and the applications—do not stand alone. The different components of the architecture pass data in an orderly manner between themselves by means of a communications fabric. One way of thinking about this fabric is in terms of the Internet and the intranet, though communications as a means to pass data actually existed long before there was an Internet and an intranet. The advent of the Internet and the intranet have led to the formalization and categorization of the types of intercommunications among the different architectural entities.

The Internet and the intranet—from the perspective of the CIF—are the lines of communication along which data flows and the different components interact with each other. Figure 8.1 shows that the Internet handles the communications that occur outside of the corporate information factory and the intranet handles those communications that occur within the confines of the CIF.

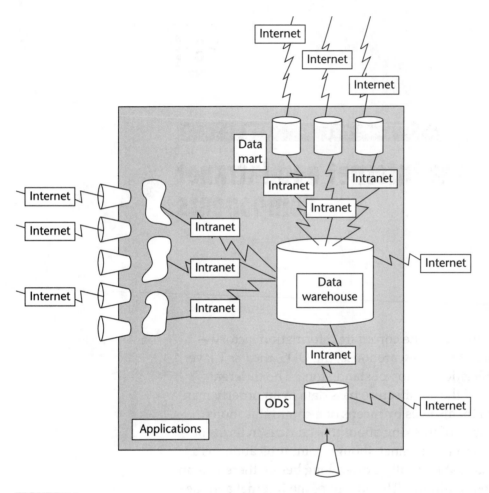

FIGURE 8.1
*The different kinds of trans-
missions within the CIF.*

The purpose of this communications fabric is to:

❏ Transport data
❏ Distribute processing
❏ Schedule and coordinate activities
❏ Notify status within the architecture
❏ Provide architectural connectivity

ISSUES OF COMMUNICATION

The communications between the different components of the CIF are governed by many factors:

❑ Volume and speed of data
❑ Network capacity, mode of transport
❑ Cost of lines
❑ Nature of the transport
❑ And availability of the communications fabric

Volume of Data

The first consideration is the volume of data that can be passed through the communications fabric, as shown in Figure 8.2.

The volume of data that must be pushed through the intranet is of great concern in the CIF because of the amount of data that is found there. The data warehouse, in particular, contains huge volumes of data that have passed from the applications or the ODS environment. In considering the proper technology for the communications fabric, the architect must first keep in mind the massive amount of data that

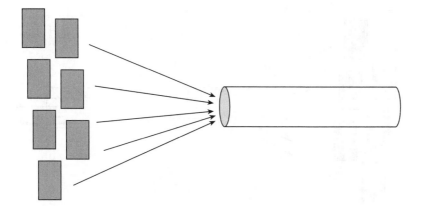

FIGURE 8.2
The volume of data to be transmitted—bandwidth—is the first parameter of interest to the CIF architect.

must pass through the environment, and the people and processes which drive the movement of data.

Speed of Data

The second consideration is the speed with which data will pass through the intranet. Figure 8.3 shows that the speed of transmission is important, because of the ODS (i.e., Class I ODS) and the need to accommodate the regular flow of massive amounts of data.

Capacity of the Network

When the rate of flow of data and the volume of data are in tandem with each other, the result is the capacity of the network. Figure 8.4 shows that network capacity for the intranet is another concern.

Mode of Transport

While capacity is a primary concern, it is not the only consideration in the overall architecture. The mode of transport is also a concern. Some communications are of a bulk type and other transmissions are of a burst type. Figure 8.5 shows these different types of transmissions.

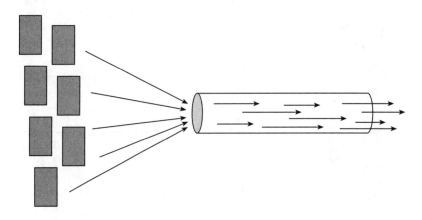

FIGURE 8.3

The speed of transmission is the second parameter of interest to the CIF architect.

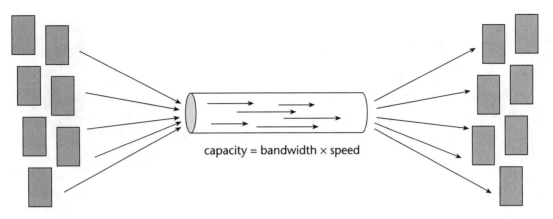

FIGURE 8.4
Line capacity is the third parameter of interest to the CIF architect.

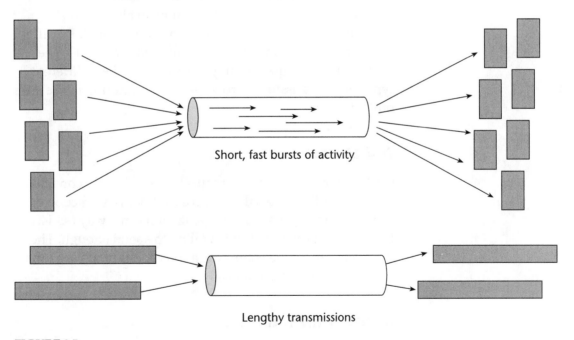

FIGURE 8.5
Some types of lines are geared for short bursts of activity; other lines are geared for bulk transmissions.

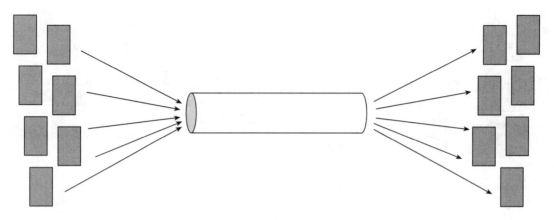

FIGURE 8.6
Cost of transmission infra-structure.

A bulk type of transmission is one where large amounts of data are transmitted all at once. The communications fabric is loaded and tied up for a lengthy amount of time as long transmissions of many bytes flow in all at once.

The burst kind of transmission is fundamentally different; in this type many short transmissions are made. The types of technologies employed to support these different types of transmissions across the communication fabric are quite distinct.

Cost of Lines

Cost is another factor the architect must take into consideration. Figure 8.6 shows that the cost of lines is a function of capacity and line type. An organization can always satisfy the needs for capacity if it is willing to spend enough. The trick is to satisfy the communications needs of the organization and to do so economically.

Nature of the Transport

Another consideration of the intranet technology is the nature of the transport. Some transport technologies are very effective at transmitting *bulk* amounts of data but are relatively expensive, difficult to set up, and difficult to maintain.

Some of the more popular networks of this type are ATM, FDDI, HPPI, and Fiber. Alternatively, other networks are very good at managing *bursts* volumes and are relatively inexpensive, easy to set up, and easy to maintain. The most popular network type in this category is Ethernet. As your solution evolves, you are likely to find a combination of these transport technologies will make up your communication fabric. The final mix will be based on your needs, and the cost and maturity of the transport technology. Figure 8.7 shows that some transport technologies are suitable for burst transmissions, while others are geared for *bulk* transmission.

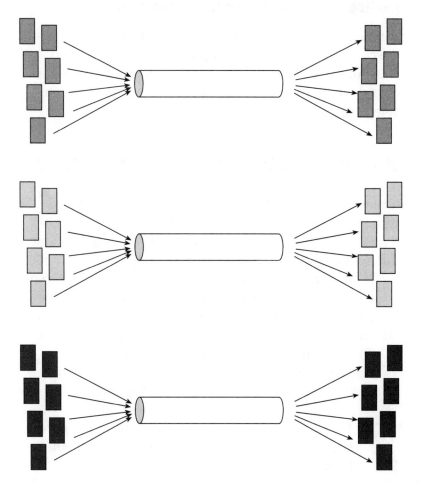

FIGURE 8.7
Different transport technologies are optimized to support different transmission needs.

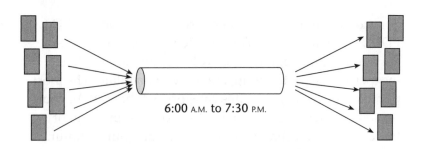

FIGURE 8.8
*The hours of availability are
yet another concern of the
CIF architect.*

6:00 A.M. to 7:30 P.M.

Availability of the Communications Fabric

A final concern of the architect is the hours of availability of
the communications fabric. Figure 8.8 depicts this issue.

All of the issues must be taken into account by the architect who is in charge of weaving together the different
components of the CIF.

WHO USES THE COMMUNICATIONS FACILITIES?

One of the interesting ways to understand the needs for
communications facilities inside and outside the CIF is in
terms of who the end users are. Figure 8.9 shows who the
different users of communications facilities are.

Direct and indirect customers are the users of the communications facilities as the data enters the CIF applications.
Once the data enters the CIF, the next set of users are farmers and explorers. As data passes out of the CIF (or into the
CIF from nondirect facilities), the end users are tourists.

Tourists, farmers, explorers, and direct users have very
different expectations when it comes to communications:

❑ **Direct customers.** Very fast, short bursts where response time is immediate, very few massive bulk
   transmissions.

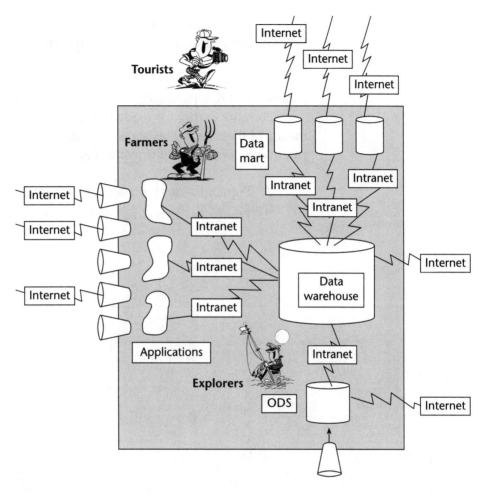

FIGURE 8.9
There are different users scattered over the landscape.

❏ **Farmers.** Short, fast bursts where response time is generally good. In some cases there is a need for a fair amount of transmission of data.

❏ **Explorers.** Very infrequent transmission of large amounts of data.

❏ **Tourists.** Sporadic transmissions of large and small amounts of data from a wide variety of sources.

Fortunately, the different classes of users are separated, and there is little overlap in the type of communications facility that is required. Figure 8.10 shows the different types of communications facilities that are required across the CIF.

A categorization of the different characteristics of the communications technologies is shown in Table 8.1.

Communications outside the CIF is accomplished by means of the Internet, as shown in Figure 8.11. There are essentially two types of transmissions that are made here:

1. Transmissions between one CIF and another CIF.
2. Transmission from a CIF to a Web site.

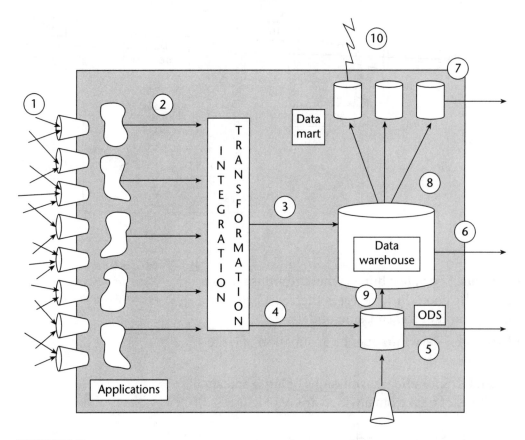

FIGURE 8.10

The different types of facilities are contained in the communications fabric.

TABLE 8.1 *Characteristics of Communications Facilities*

	Speed	Volume	Capacity	Facility Type
1. Entry into applications	high	moderate	moderate	burst
2. Applications to I & T	high	high	very high	bulk
3. I & T to DW	high	high	very high	bulk
4. I & T to ODS	very high	low	high	burst
5. ODS to DSS	low	low	low	bulk & burst
6. DW to DSS	low	low	low	bulk
7. Data mart to DSS	very low	very low	very low	burst
8. DW to data mart	low	moderate/low	moderate/low	bulk
9. ODS to DW	low	moderate/low	low	bulk
10. Internet	low	low	low	burst

Each of these types of transmissions has its own set of characteristics.

A CIF to CIF transmission may be one where one corporation is communicating with another corporation, or one where two parts of the same corporation are in communica-

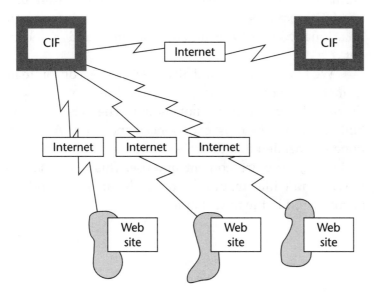

FIGURE 8.11
The Internet connections.

tion where the two parts of the corporation are served by different CIFs.

SUMMARY

The communications between the different components of the CIF are accomplished by means of Internet and intranet transmissions. Intranet transmissions are those that occur within the CIF. Internet transmissions are those that occur from/to the CIF and other external agencies. Some of the architectural issues are:

- ❑ The volume of data to be transported
- ❑ The speed of transmission
- ❑ The total capacity of transmission
- ❑ The mode of transmission
- ❑ The cost of transmission

Different types of users have different transmission needs. Farmers are found in the data marts, the data warehouse and ODS, explorers are found in the data warehouse and occasionally in the ODS, and tourists are found on the Internet.

We have now covered all aspects of the corporate information factory necessary to give end users visibility into the data. However, this is not enough. The data lacks legibility to all but the most experienced end users. A final component is needed that describes the data in terms of definition, structure, content, and use. This component of the corporate information factory is the metadata and will be discussed in the next chapter.

9

The Metadata Component

The most important yet most ambiguous, most amorphous component of the CIF is the metadata. From the standpoint of cohesiveness and continuity of structure across the many different components of the corporate information factory, metadata is easily the most important component.

WHAT IS METADATA?

A very common way of thinking about metadata is that it is data about data. An alternate way of describing metadata is that it is everything about data needed to promote its administration and use. These two widely accepted definitions of metadata, however, do not do justice to what metadata really is. A more practical approach to describing metadata is through citing some examples:

- ❏ **Data layout.** Describing the relative position and format of data in a storage media—customer record.

    - ❏ Cust-id   char (15)
    - ❏ Cust-name   varchar (45)

139

❏ Cust-address   varchar (45)

❏ Cust-balance   dec fixed (15, 2)

❏ **Content.** There are 150,000 occurrences of transaction X in table PLK.

❏ **Indexes.** Table XYZ has indexes on the following columns:

❏ Column HYT

❏ Column BFD

❏ Column MJI

❏ **Refreshment scheduling.** Table ABC is refreshed every Tuesday at 2:00 P.M.

❏ **Usage.** Only 2 of the 10 columns in table ABC have been used over the past six months.

❏ **Referential integrity.** Table XYZ is related to table ABC by means of the key QWE.

❏ **General documentation.** "Table ABC was designed in 1975 as part of the new accounts payable system. Table ABC contains accounts overdue data as calculated by . . . ."

These examples of metadata only begin to scratch the surface of the possibilities. The final form will only be limited by your imagination and those needs that govern the use and administration of the corporate information factory.

The reason why metadata is so important to the corporate information factory, and its different components, is that metadata is the glue that holds the architecture together. Figure 9.1 illustrates this role of metadata.

Without metadata, the different components of the CIF are merely standalone structures with no relationship to any other structure. It is metadata that gives the different structures—components of the architecture—an overall cohesiveness. Through metadata, one component of the architecture is able to interpret and make sense of what another component is trying to communicate.

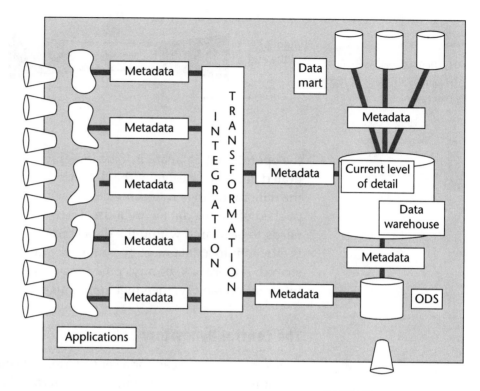

FIGURE 9.1
*Metadata is the glue that
holds the different components of the CIF together.
Without metadata there
would be no cohesiveness
across the CIF.*

THE CONFLICT WITHIN METADATA

For all of the benefits of metadata, there is a conflict: Metadata has a need to be shared, and a propensity to be managed and used, in an autonomous manner. Unfortunately,
these propensities are in direct conflict with each other.
Equally unfortunate is that the pull of metadata is *very, very*
strong in both directions at the same time. Because of this
conflict metadata can be thought of as polarized, as shown
in Figure 9.2.

Because the pull is so strong and so diametrically opposite, metadata is sometimes said to be *schizophrenic*. This
leads to some fairly extreme conflicts within the CIF. As an
example of the propensity of metadata to be shared, consider an architect who is building an operational database. If

FIGURE 9.2
Metadata is stretched by two opposing forces.

the operational database is to be integrated, the basic integrated, modeled design of the data needs to be shared from the data modeling environment. As the data ages and is pushed off to the data warehouse, the structure of the data needs to be shared within the data warehouse. As the data is moved into a data mart, the data once again needs to be shared. If there is to be any consistency across the corporate information factory, then metadata must be shared.

The Central Repository

In response to the need for a central, unified source of data definition, structure, content, and use across the corporate information factory, the notion of a central repository arises (Figure 9.3).

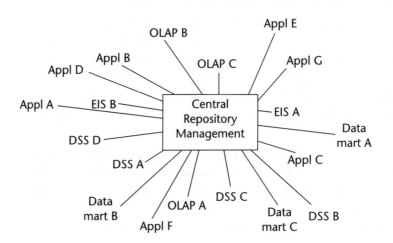

FIGURE 9.3
One approach to managing metadata is the data dictionary or the central repository approach.

The central repository approach is a good solution to the needs for sharability of metadata. Although the argument for sharability cannot be denied, is a central repository the answer to the organization's needs?

Consider the scenario of a DSS analyst working on Lotus 1-2-3 who is deep into solving an analytical problem. At 2:17 A.M. the DSS analyst has a brain storm and makes changes to the Lotus spreadsheet. Does the analyst need to call the data warehouse administrator and ask permission to define and analyze a new data structure? Does the DSS analyst need permission to derive a new data element on-the-fly? Shouldn't this new data structure and new data element be documented in the metadata repository?

Of course, the DSS analyst does not need or want anyone telling him or her what can and cannot be done at an early morning hour in the middle of a creative analysis of a problem. The DSS analyst operates in a state of autonomy and the central repository is neither welcome nor effective. The repository simply gets in the way of the DSS analyst using Lotus 1-2-3. The DSS analyst does what is needed to bypass the repository, usually ignoring updates to the metadata in the repository.

The need for autonomy at the DSS analysis level is so overwhelming and the tools of DSS access and analysis are so powerful that a central repository does not stand a chance as a medium for total metadata management.

Is Autonomy the Answer?

If a powerful case can be made for why a central repository is not the answer, consider the opposite of the central repository: where everybody "does their own thing," as seen in Figure 9.4.

In the figure, there is autonomy in that every environment and every tool has its own unique facility for interpreting metadata. Because there are no constraints of any type anywhere in the environment, there is complete auton-

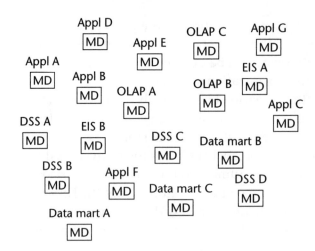

FIGURE 9.4

The autonomous approach to metadata management.

omy. The autonomy suggested by the figure is pleasing to the DSS analyst in that there is no one or no authority telling the DSS analyst what to do. However, the following questions arise:

❑ What happens when one DSS user wants to know how data is defined and used elsewhere?

❑ What happens when a DSS user wants to know what a unit of data means?

❑ What happens when one DSS user wants to correlate his results with another DSS analyst?

❑ What happens when a DSS analyst needs to reconcile results with the source systems providing the data for analysis?

❑ What happens when data is not interpreted consistently? What profit figures are correct?

The result is chaos. There simply is no uniformity or cohesiveness anywhere to be found in the autonomous environment. The purely autonomous environment is as impractical and unworkable as the central repository environment. Neither approach is acceptable, in the long run, to the architect wanting to make the corporate information factory a professionally organized environment.

In order to be successful, the CIF architect must balance the legitimate need to share metadata with the need for autonomy. Understanding the problem is the first step to a solution. In order to achieve a balance, a different perspective of metadata is required.

The structure for metadata suggested in Figure 9.5 states that there needs to be a separation of metadata at each component in the architecture between metadata that is sharable and metadata that is autonomous. Metadata must be divided at each component of the CIF:

❏ At the application level

❏ At the ODS

❏ At the data warehouse

❏ At the data mart

Furthermore, all metadata at an individual node must also fit into either a shared or autonomous category. There can be no metadata that is neither sharable nor autonomous. Likewise, metadata cannot be sharable and autonomous at the same time.

But Figure 9.5 has other ramifications. The metadata that is managed at an individual component must be accessible by tools that reside at that component. The tools may

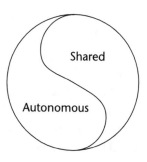

FIGURE 9.5
The metadata within each component is either shared or autonomous. The categories are mutually exclusive.

be tools of access, analysis, or development. In any case, whether the metadata is sharable or autonomous, the metadata needs to be available to and usable by the different tools that reside at the architectural component.

Another implication of the figure is that sharable metadata needs to be able to be replicated from one architectural component to another. Once the sharable metadata is replicated, it can be used and incorporated into the processing that occurs at other components of the corporate information factory.

Differentiating between Sharable and Autonomous Metadata

The following are examples of typical sharable data:

- ❏ Table name and attributes might be shared among applications and the data warehouse.
- ❏ Some definitions of data will be shared between the enterprise data model and the data warehouse and the data mart.
- ❏ Physical attributes might be shared among the applications and the ODS.
- ❏ Physical attributes might be shared from one application to another.
- ❏ And all of the above need to be shared with the I & T layer.

Ultimately, very commonly used metadata needs to be sharable.

An example of autonomous metadata might be the indexes a table has for its use in an application. At the data mart level, the results of a given analysis might be autonomous. At the data warehouse level, the metrics of the content of a table may well be autonomous data. At the ODS level, the response time achieved in access and analysis of the ODS is a form of autonomous metadata. In short, there are many and varied forms of autonomous metadata. In general, there is much more autonomous metadata than there is shared metadata.

A SYSTEM OF RECORD

In order to make the structure workable as suggested in Figure 9.5, there needs to be a clear and formal definition of the system of record (i.e., authoritative source) for shared metadata (Figure 9.6). The system of record for shared metadata implies that each shared metadata element must be owned and maintained by only one component of the corporate information factory (e.g., data warehouse or data mart or ODS, etc.). In contrast, this shared metadata can be replicated for use by all components of the corporate information factory.

For example, suppose that the definition of shared metadata is made at the data warehouse level (a very normal assumption). The implication is that the definition can be used throughout the CIF, but cannot be altered anywhere except at the data warehouse. In other words, the data mart DSS analyst can use the metadata but cannot alter the metadata.

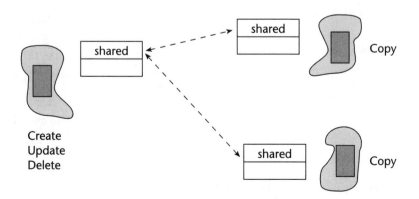

Create
Update
Delete

FIGURE 9.6
The system of record for the metadata.

Establishing the system of record for metadata is a defining factor in the successful implementation and evolution of the CIF. Another important implication of the approach to distributed metadata is that there be an exchange of this meta object among the different architectural components (Figure 9.7).

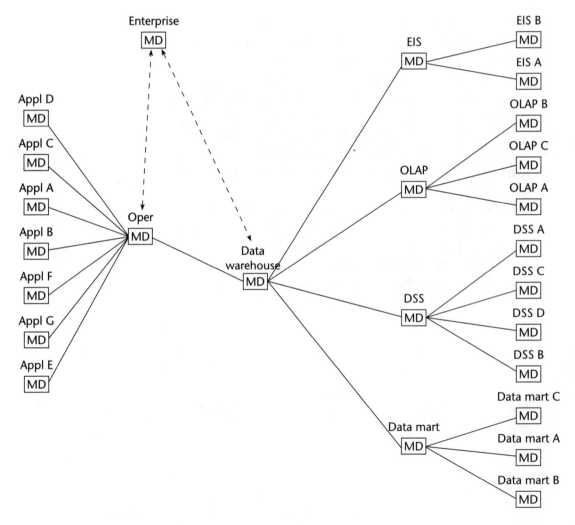

FIGURE 9.7
Metadata needs to be exchanged across the many different components of the CIF.

The sharable meta object needs to be passed efficiently and on an on-demand basis. One of the more important implications of this sharability is that it be shared across multiple technologies as illustrated in Figure 9.8.

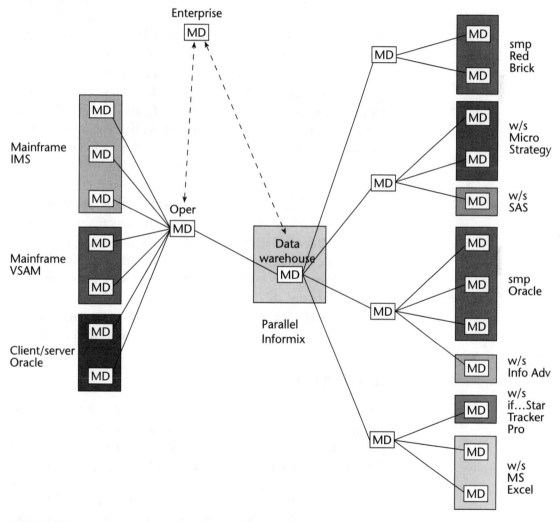

FIGURE 9.8

One of the main challenges of sharing metadata across the CIF is that there are many different platforms to be serviced.

The whole notion of sharing metadata across different components of the architecture along with the autonomy of metadata at each component level results in a larger architecture. The larger picture shown in Figure 9.9 shows that there is indeed a balance between sharability and autonomy. With this architecture, the end user has all the autonomy desired, and the CIF architect has all the sharability and uniformity of definition that is desired. The conflict between sharability and autonomy that is evident in metadata is resolved quite nicely by the architecture outlined in Figure 9.9.

Consider the usage of this architecture in Figure 9.10, where a DSS analyst at the data mart level desires to know more about the origin of attribute ABC in table XYZ. The data mart analyst recognizes that there is available sharable information about table XYZ. The DSS analyst asks the data warehouse what information is available. The data warehouse offers sharable information about the table and the attribute in question. If the DSS analyst has what is needed, the question is resolved. If the DSS analyst is still unsure about the table and the attributes, he will push further into the network of sharable metadata and go back to the application. The DSS analyst then learns even more about the metadata in question. If there are still further questions, the DSS analyst can look inside the I & T layer or even go back to the enterprise model to see more information about the table and attribute.

Impact Analysis

Another use of sharable metadata is that of impact analysis (Figure 9.11). In the figure, an application programmer is getting ready to make a change to some part of the application. The CIF architect will ask the following questions:

❑ When was the change made in the application?
❑ What elements of data are going to be affected across the CIF?

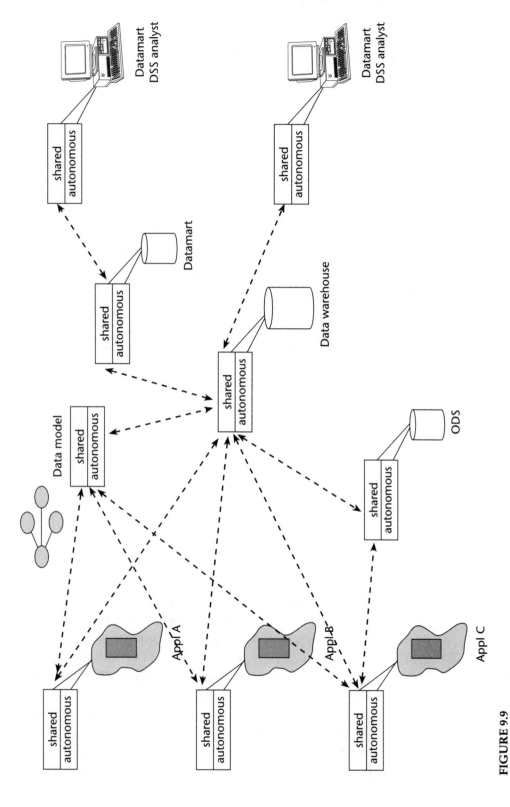

FIGURE 9.9

A larger metadata architecture that balances sharability and autonomy.

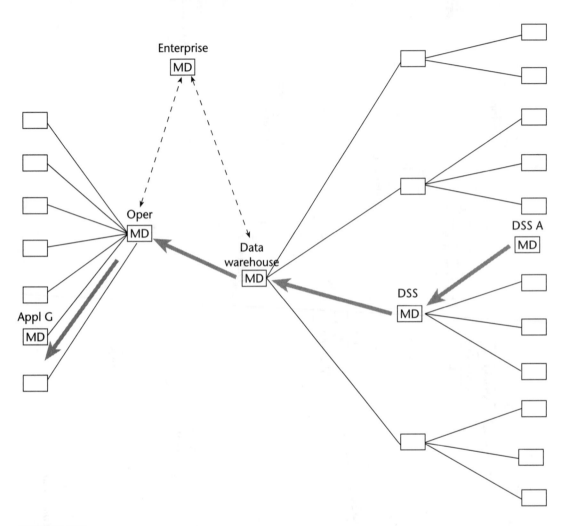

FIGURE 9.10

Metadata information all the way back to the applications environment is available to the DSS analyst at the data mart, if needed.

With the formalized structure of metadata, it is a relatively simple matter to determine what data in what environment will be impacted by a change in the applications environment.

As another example of the usage of the distributed metadata architecture, consider the circumstances depicted in Figure 9.12.

A DSS analyst in the data mart environment wants to know what data constitutes the source for data that has arrived in the data mart. In other words, for a data element entry in the data mart, what data at the application source

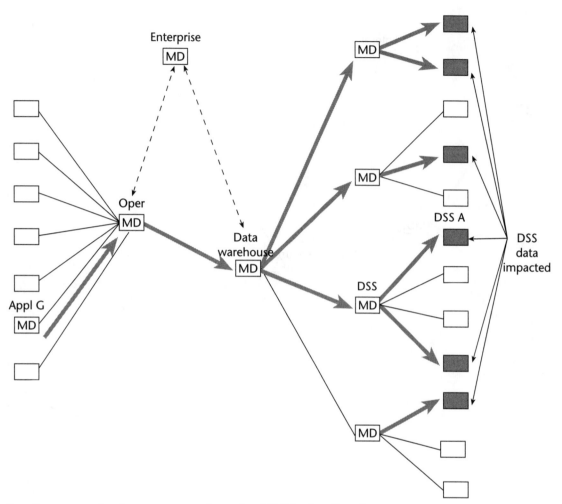

level was required to generate the value? With the distributed network of shared metadata, there is a straightforward way of making the analysis.

Metadata in the Decision-Support System and Operational Environment

Metadata plays a very different role in the DSS and the operational environments. After a short period of time, driving a familiar route, drivers take road signs for granted and ignore their information because it's simply not needed.

FIGURE 9.11
One important use of distributed metadata is the ability to do impact analysis. In this case, the applications programmer has asked the question, "If there is a change in the applications data, which data marts are affected?"

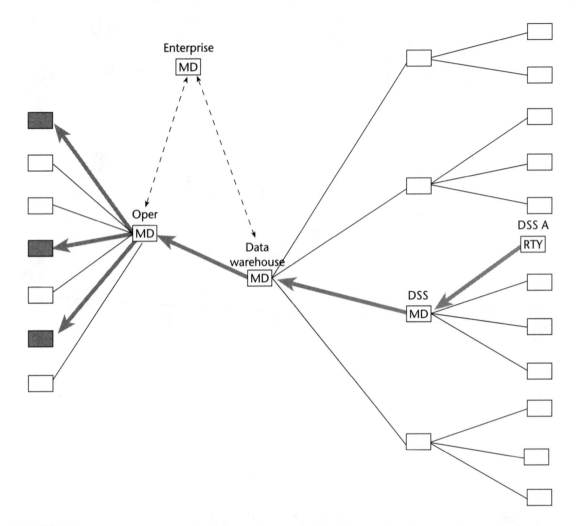

FIGURE 9.12

In this case, a data mart analyst wants to know the origins of data element RTY. Distributed metadata allows the DSS analyst to trace RTY to its origins.

If the same activity is repeated over and over, metadata can get in the way of the end user. After the tenth time that an end user repeats the same activity, the end user hardly glances at whatever metadata is present and may even complain that the display of metadata gets in the way of doing his or her job.

However, when drivers are in unfamiliar territory, road signs make all the difference in the world. The same can be said for metadata in the DSS environment. When the DSS analyst is doing a *new* report, metadata is invaluable in telling the DSS analyst what he or she needs to know to get started and do effective DSS analysis. Metadata plays an entirely different role in the world of DSS than it does in the world of operational systems.

Because of this difference, it is worth noting how metadata relates to the CIF based on the differences between operational processing and DSS processing. Figure 9.13 shows that metadata in the operational environment is a by-product of processing. In fact, metadata in the operational environment is of most use to the developer and the

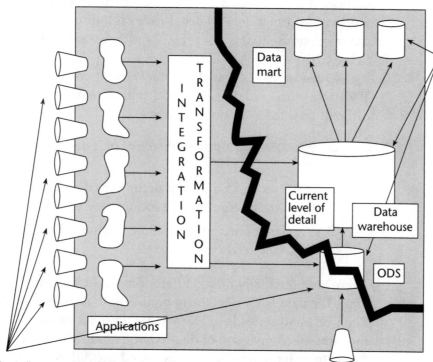

The influence of metadata is very strong and is important to the DSS analyst in doing the day-to-day job.

The influence of metadata is passive and is of primary importance to the developer and the maintenance personnel.

FIGURE 9.13
The role metadata plays throughout the CIF is quite different.

designer. Metadata in the DSS environment, on the other hand, is of great use to the DSS analyst as an active part of the analytical, informational effort. This is due largely to the fact that, in this environment, the end user has more control over how data is interpreted and used.

VERSIONING OF METADATA

One of the characteristics of the data warehouse environment is that it contains a robust supply of historical information. It is not unusual for it to contain 5- to 10-years worth of information. As such, history is a dimension of the data warehouse that is not present or important elsewhere in the CIF.

Consider the DSS analyst who is trying to compare 1996 data with 1990 data. The DSS analyst may be having a difficult time for a variety of reasons:

❑ 1996 data had a different source of data than 1990 data.

❑ 1996 data had a different definition of product than 1990 data's definition of product.

❑ 1996 had a different marketing territory than 1990's marketing territory.

There are potentially many different factors which may make the data from 1996 incompatible with data from 1990. The DSS analyst needs to know what those factors are if a meaningful comparison of data is to be made across the years. In order to be able to understand the difference in information across the years, the DSS analyst needs to see metadata that is *versioned*.

Versioned metadata is metadata that is tracked over time. Figure 9.14 shows that as changes are made to data over time, those changes are reflected in the metadata as different versions of metadata are created.

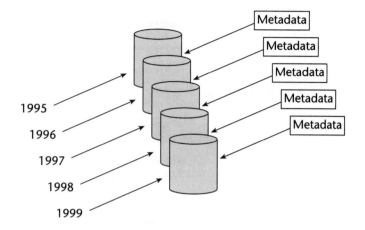

FIGURE 9.14
Versions of metadata must be kept in order to track changes in data structure that naturally occur in the data warehouse.

One of the characteristics of versioned metadata is that each occurrence of it contains a from-date and a to-date, resulting in a continuous *state* record.

Once the continuous versions of metadata are created, the DSS analyst can use those versions to understand content of data in its historical context. For example, the DSS analyst solicits answers to such key questions as:

❏ On December 29, 1995, what was the source of data for file XYZ?

❏ On October 14, 1996, what was the definition of a product?

❏ On July 20, 1994, what was the price of product ABC?

Versioned metadata for the data warehouse adds an extremely important dimension of data.

Metadata and Archiving

In the same vein as versioned metadata, the CIF architect must consider the role of metadata as it is archived. When data is removed from the data warehouse, data mart, or the

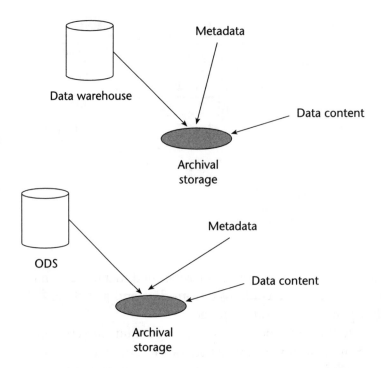

FIGURE 9.15
When data is archived, meta-data is stored directly on the archival medium with the actual data content.

ODS environment, it can be discarded or, more likely, archived onto secondary storage. As this happens, it makes sense to store the metadata relating to the archived data along with the archived data. By doing this, the CIF architect ensures that at a later point in time, archival information will be available in the most efficient and effective manner. Figure 9.15 shows that metadata should be stored with the archival information.

CAPTURING METADATA

The Achilles heel of metadata has always been in its capture. When applications were built in the 1960s, there was no documentation or captured metadata. Organizations realized in the late 1980s and early 1990s that no metadata existed for the systems that were written years ago. Trying to go back in time and reconstruct metadata that was attached to systems that were written decades ago was a daunting task. The obstacles of trying to reconstruct metadata 20 years after the fact were many:

1. The people who wrote the systems originally were not available because:
   ❑ They had been promoted.
   ❑ They had left for another job.
   ❑ They had forgotten.
   ❑ They never understood the data in the first place.

2. Budget for development had dried up years ago. Trying to show management tangible benefits from a data dictionary project or a repository project required a huge imagination on the part of the manager footing the bill.

3. Physically gathering the metadata information was its own challenge. In many cases, source code had been lost a long time ago.

4. Even if metadata could be recovered from an old application system, only some metadata was available. A complete picture of metadata was almost impossible to reconstruct.

5. Even if metadata could be recovered from an old legacy system, as updates were made to the system, keeping the updates in synch with the metadata manager—a dictionary or a repository—was almost impossible.

For these reasons and more, capturing applications metadata after the fact is a very difficult thing to do.

A much better alternative is the capturing of metadata during the active development process. When a tool of automation is used for the development process and is able to produce metadata as a by-product of its code that is pro-

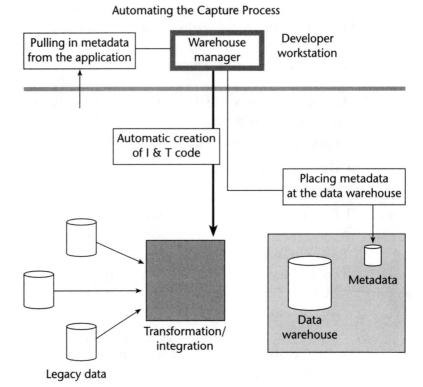

Automating the Capture Process

FIGURE 9.16

Capturing metadata to support integration and transformation. The same process can apply for development and capture in the application environment.

Metadata is developed as an interactive product of designing and developing the data warehouse environment:

    It is complete.

    It is done every time.

    It is done automatically.

    It is not an afterthought.

    It is not optional.

    It requires no extra effort—manually or otherwise.

duced, then there is the possibility of creating metadata automatically.

Figure 9.16 shows a tool which produces metadata as a by-product of the creation of code. There are many advantages to this approach:

❏ Metadata creation does not require another budgetary line item—it comes automatically.

❏ Update of metadata as changes are made is not a problem.

❏ Metadata versions are created every time a new version of code is created.

❏ Programmers do not know that they are creating metadata.

❏ Programmers think they are building systems. The creation of the metadata comes spontaneously, unknown to the programmer.

❏ Logic of transformation can be trapped. The transformation tool is able to understand exactly what conversion and reformatting logic is occurring.

The automatic creation of code offers many advantages in the capture of metadata—ultimately, productivity.

META PROCESS INFORMATION

While metadata is undoubtedly the center of attention in the CIF, there are other types of meta objects. One such type of meta object is metaprocess information. While metadata is descriptive data about data, metaprocess information is descriptive information about code or process. Metaprocess information is useful anywhere there is a large body of code. The three most obvious places in the CIF where this occurs are:

1. At the I & T layer.
2. Within the applications.
3. As data passes to the data mart from the data warehouse.

Uses at the Integration and Transformation Layer

The I & T layer metaprocess information is interesting to the DSS analyst as he or she tries to determine how a unit of data was derived from the applications. When the DSS analyst looks at a value of $275 in the data warehouse and sees that the source value was $314, he or she needs to know what was going on in terms of processing logic inside the I & T interface. The DSS analyst needs to see metaprocess information about the I & T interface.

Uses within Applications

Within the applications, much editing, capture, and update of data occurs. The analyst who will specify the steps needed for integration needs to know what processing will occur in the applications. This description is metaprocess information.

Uses from the Data Warehouse to the Data Mart

As data passes from the data warehouse to the data mart, it is customized and summarized to meet the individual demands of the department to which it is being shipped. This process is very interesting to the DSS analyst who must do drill-down processing. In drill-down processing, the DSS analyst goes to successively lower levels of detail in order to explain to management how a unit of summarization came to be. The DSS analyst, or the tool he or she is using, occasionally needs to drill down past the data mart into the data warehouse. At this point, the DSS analyst needs to see metaprocess information about the interface between the data mart and the data warehouse.

SUMMARY

Metadata is the glue that holds the CIF together. Without metadata, the CIF is just a collection of components that manage and use data with no continuity or cohesiveness.

Metadata presents different challenges in that it needs to be both autonomous and sharable at the same time. Unfortunately, these goals are mutually exclusive. In order to be successful, however, both goals need to be simultaneously achieved.

One approach to sharability is through a central repository. It satisfies many of the needs for sharability, but does not satisfy the need for autonomy. Another approach to autonomy of metadata is for "everyone to do their own thing." This approach achieves autonomy, but there is no sharability.

An alternate approach is *distributed* metadata. In distributed metadata, some data is shared and other metadata is autonomous. There needs to be a rigorously defined system of record (i.e., authoritative source) for the shared portion of distributed metadata.

One of the challenges of shared metadata is that of crossing many different lines of technology. Another challenge is the transport of meta objects.

Metadata plays a very different role in the operational environment than it does in the DSS environment. In the operational environment, the applications developer is the primary user of metadata. In the DSS environment, the end user is the primary user of metadata.

This completes our discussion on the architectural components that comprise the corporate information factory and how they should be ideally implemented. In the next chapter, we will discuss variations to implementing the CIF architecture and the associated risks to the long-term viability of your information ecosystem.

10

C H A P T E R T E N

Variations to the Corporate Information Factory

A policeman won't blow his whistle and arrest you if you violate the design guidelines of the corporate information factory. However, when you choose to build your systems outside of the architecture suggested by the CIF, there is a price to pay. In some cases, the price is a large one; in others, it is not. As long as the architect is aware of the stakes and the potential disadvantages of a design that violates the CIF, there is no reason why the architect must follow the CIF design.

The CIF and its different components have been specified as they are for a reason. If they are built in a manner other than that outlined in this book, something important may suffer. This chapter will suggest several popular alternatives to the CIF and point out the price for not having followed the design principles specified.

SHOULD WE BUILD THE DATA MART OR THE DATA WAREHOUSE FIRST?

The classical structure for delivering business intelligence contains two levels of data that are of interest—the data

165

warehouse data and the data mart data. The data warehouse, often called the *current level of detail,* contains the bulk of the detailed data that has been collected and integrated from the applications environment.

The data mart is a departmental subset of the current detailed data that is shaped to meet the DSS processing needs of that particular department. The source of data mart data is the data warehouse. Figure 10.1 shows the relationship between the data warehouse and the data mart.

The data mart—sometimes called the ROLAP or the MOLAP environment—contains a subset of the current level data that has been customized for the department. Typically, the finance, marketing, and sales departments have their own data marts. The data mart usually contains data that has been distilled to meet the performance, analytic, navigation, and visualization needs of a particular department. Data marts are generally very small compared to the data warehouse. This is due to the fact that data marts generally contain sample or subset data, or data that has been aggregated by predefined set business dimensions (e.g., product, time, channel, etc.) and metrics (revenue, profit, usage, counts, etc.).

The data warehouse contains a massive amount of integrated data and represents a truly corporate understanding

FIGURE 10.1

The relationship between the data warehouse and the data mart.

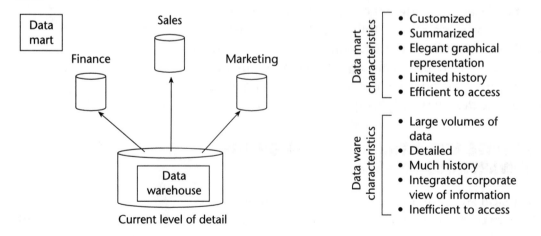

of information. Because of the massive volumes of data found in the data warehouse, and since it serves many different departmental data marts, the data warehouse is not terribly efficient to access.

One of the most important questions the data warehouse architect faces is that of the order in which to build the data marts and the data warehouse. There are two basic choices:

1. Build the data marts before the data warehouse is built.
2. Build the data marts in conjunction with the data warehouse.

The decision to do one or the other does not *appear* to be an important decision, but this decision is one of the most important and strategic decisions that the architect will ever make. The CIF dictates that the data marts be built in conjunction with the data warehouse, but there is nothing to keep the data marts from being built first, directly from the applications environment.

Building the Data Mart First

One choice the CIF architect has is to build the data marts first, directly from the applications environment.

The data mart shown in Figure 10.2 is built directly from the applications. When the diagram is as simple as that shown in the figure, there is no problem with the building of the data mart as the first part of the architecture. Building the data mart directly from the applications first appears to be cheap, easy, and fast.

There are then some very real reasons why building the data marts directly from applications is a poor idea; the price to pay is severe. It is not at all obvious at the moment of building the first one or two data marts. Instead, the price becomes obvious as soon as the third or fourth data mart is

Applications

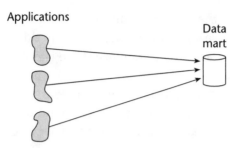

FIGURE 10.2
Building the data mart directly from the applications.

being built. It takes a while for the organization to discover that there is a tremendous price to the building of the data mart in a manner not suggested by the CIF. This price is usually paid as the complexity of the interface increases, or when considering placement and interpretation of data. We will discuss this price shortly.

Building the Data Mart in Conjunction with the Data Warehouse

The alternative to building data marts as the first part of the architecture is to build the data warehouse first, then build the data marts on top of the data warehouse (Figure 10.3). This alternative is expensive, slow, and difficult. Compared to the ease of building data marts directly from the applications first, it is reasonable to ask why anyone would choose this approach.

Applications

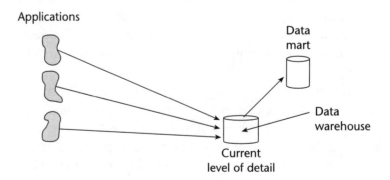

FIGURE 10.3
Building the data mart from the data warehoused data.

Program

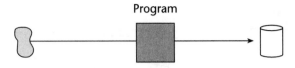

FIGURE 10.4
The interface program must be written, maintained, and executed.

Complexity of the Interface   In order to answer this question, let's shift focus to the interface between the applications and the data mart or the data warehouse itself. In Figures 10.2 and 10.3, there is a simple line that represents the flow of data from the applications to the data mart or to the data warehouse. The interface shown in Figure 10.4 is anything but simple. Rather, a program must be written, maintained, and provided resources every time it is executed.

In short, much development and mechanical resources are required every time the line between the program and the data mart or the data warehouse appears.

The resources required by the interface become more relevant when we consider that the environment depicted for the data mart and the data warehouse is hardly realistic. The diagrams shown in Figures 10.2 and 10.3 represent the world of business intelligence when the *first* data mart is built, not the world when the *last* data mart is built. In order to picture the more realistic and mature environment of data marts and applications, Figure 10.5 shows that there are many source applications and many data marts; each of the data marts has its own user or department.

By the same token, when the data warehouse is built first, there are multiple sources of data and multiple data marts that will be built in conjunction, as seen in Figure 10.6.

The reality of this environment is that there are many application sources and many data marts that will be built. The perspective shown in Figures 10.2 and 10.3 is merely the perspective of the very first of the data marts that will be built. As such, the environment shown in these figures is an extremely short-term view of the world.

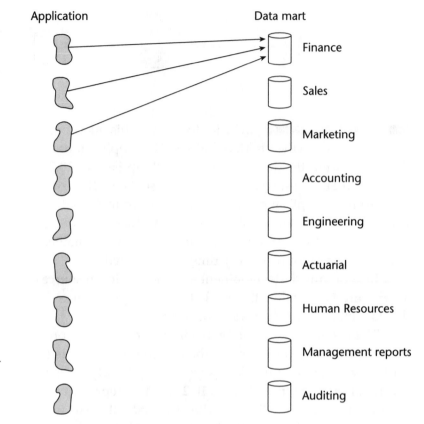

Application   Data mart

Finance

Sales

Marketing

Accounting

Engineering

Actuarial

Human Resources

Management reports

Auditing

FIGURE 10.5

A much more accurate picture of the information environment where there are many applications and data marts.

Figure 10.7 shows that the interface between the applications and the data marts is a very complex one. There are *many* programs that interface the two environments that must be built and maintained. In addition, the amount of hardware required to move the data along all of the interfaces is considerable. In fact, the number of interfaces required can be expressed mathematically. If there are m applications and if there are n data marts, then $m \times n$ interfaces will have to be built and executed.

The scenario described in Figure 10.7 is one that is reminiscent of the classical operational *spider web environment.*

The complexity and chaos of the direct-to-data-mart approach is in stark contrast to the order and discipline that

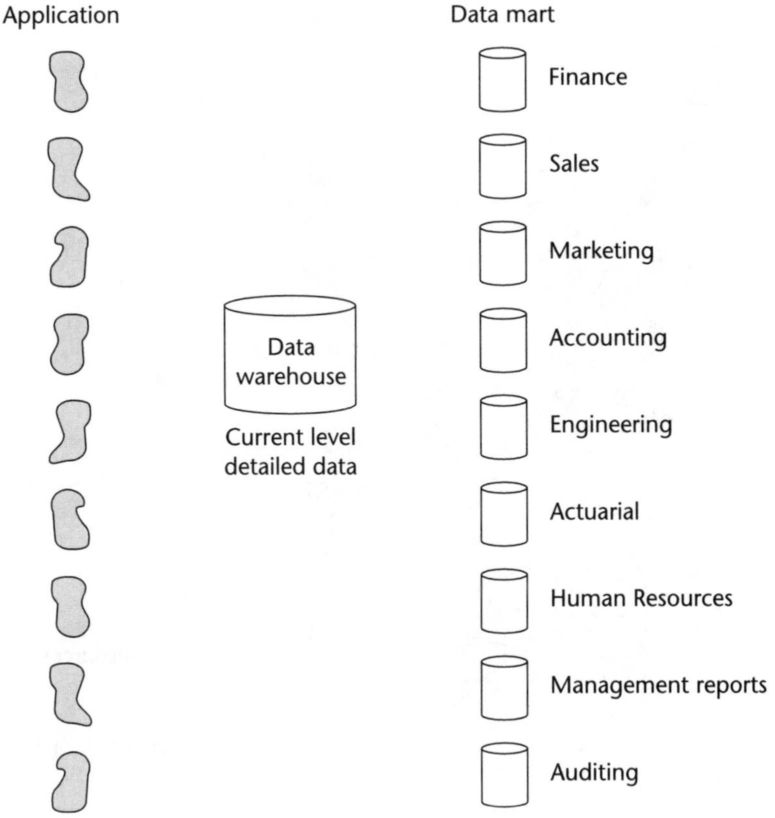

Application

Data mart

Finance

Sales

Marketing

Accounting

Data warehouse

Engineering

Current level detailed data

Actuarial

Human Resources

Management reports

Auditing

FIGURE 10.6
A much more accurate picture of the information environment where there are many applications and data marts integrated via the data warehouse.

is achieved by building the data mart in conjunction with the data warehouse. Figure 10.8 displays this alternative.

There are, of course, interfaces that are required in the building of the data warehouse first. However, there is a very orderly approach to their building that can be achieved, as seen in Figure 10.8. The number of interfaces that are required can be expressed mathematically. If there are m applications and there are n data marts, then building the data warehouse in conjunction with the data mart requires $m + n$ interfaces.

Since the direct data mart approach requires $m \times n$ interfaces and the data warehouse approach requires $m + n$ interfaces, the conclusion can be drawn that the more com-

Application

Data mart

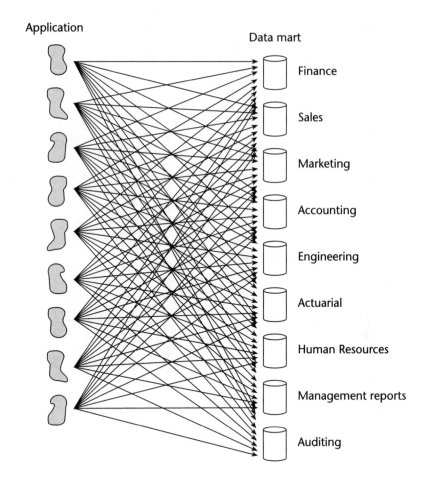

Finance

Sales

Marketing

Accounting

Engineering

Actuarial

Human Resources

Management reports

Auditing

FIGURE 10.7

The interfaces between applications and data marts. If there are m *applications and* n *data marts, there will be* m ×n *interface programs.*

plex and larger the application environment and the more data marts there will be, the more complex the interface between the data mart and the application becomes. Indeed, the complexity increases geometrically with an increase in scale.

Placement of Data   The interfaces between the different environments is not the only reason why building the data marts directly from the applications environment is a bad idea. A second reason is because of the dilemma caused by where to place common and unique data.

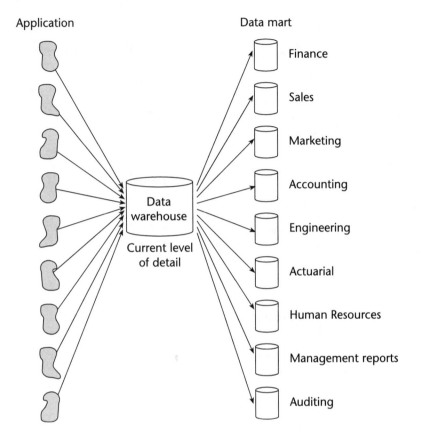

Application

Data mart

Finance

Sales

Marketing

Accounting

Engineering

Actuarial

Human Resources

Management reports

Auditing

Data warehouse

Current level of detail

FIGURE 10.8
The interfaces between the applications and the data warehouse and the data warehouse and the data mart. If there are m applications and n data marts, there will be m + n interface programs.

Figure 10.9 shows that the data warehouse is a very convenient place to hold the common corporate data. The data marts are good places to hold the data that is unique to the department that owns the mart. The architecture shown in Figure 10.9 provides for a clean and convenient positioning of corporate and departmental data.

Figure 10.10 shows that where data marts are built directly from the applications, there is a need for placing common corporate data in every data mart.

Each data mart contains its own collection of unique data and common detailed data. The massive redundancy of data that results from every data mart "doing its own thing" is seen in Figure 10.11.

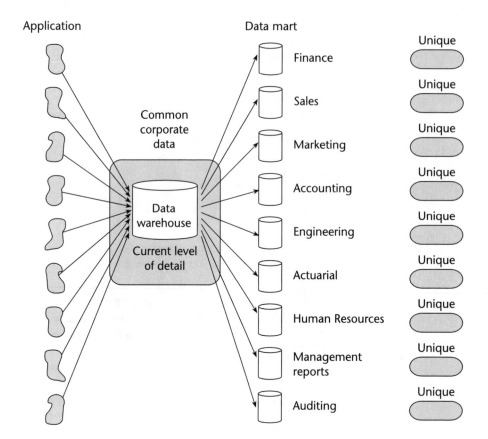

FIGURE 10.9

There is a very nice division between common corporate data and departmentally unique data.

Common data is grossly redundant across the different data marts. Furthermore, the data that is redundant is the most voluminous of all the data a corporation has. This is a very expensive proposition from both a data storage and processing perspective.

Interpreting Number of Customers   There is yet another reason why building the data marts directly from the applications is a bad idea and that reason is illustrated by asking the question, "How many customers does the corporation have?" Figure 10.12 shows that where the data marts are built directly from the applications that each different department has its own answer to the question of how many

Application

Data mart

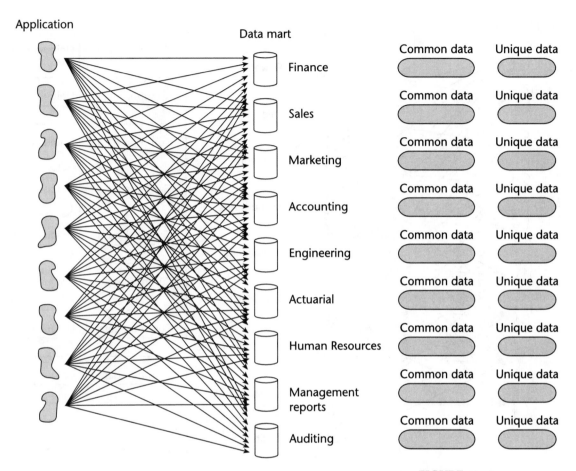

FIGURE 10.10
Where data is moved directly into the data mart, there is a mixture of both common corporate and department unique data.

customers. Trying to make a coherent business decision based on the wildly differing interpretations of how many customers is impossible.

Contrast the chaos of Figure 10.12 with the discipline seen in Figure 10.13.

Figure 10.13 shows that in the current level of detail there is a single definition and a single occurrence of a customer; in each customer record there is a single, integrated definition of what a customer is. The record for a customer has qualifying attributes that allow the distinction to be made between different classes of customers. The attributes

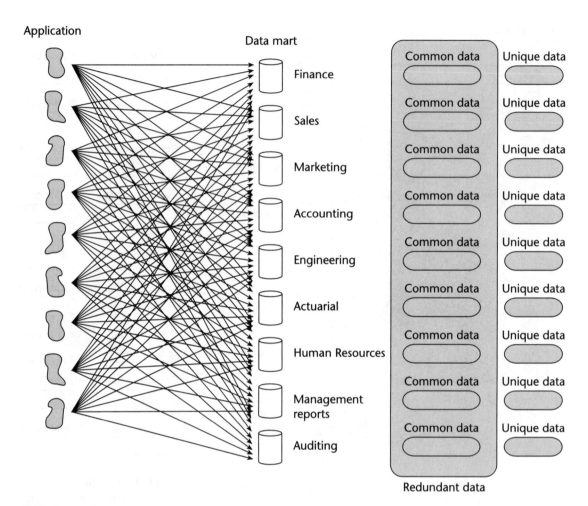

Application

Data mart

Finance

Sales

Marketing

Accounting

Engineering

Actuarial

Human Resources

Management reports

Auditing

Common data   Unique data

Redundant data

FIGURE 10.11

There is a massive amount of redundant data.

typically contain data about old, new, and potential customers, about large and small customers, about Italian, English, American customers, and so forth. Because there is a single integrated definition, the departments can clearly identify exactly what category of customer is being considered, something that is not possible when the data marts are built directly from the applications.

Once the departments can tell what data they are talking about, making distinctions between the different categories of customers is easy. Once the distinction between

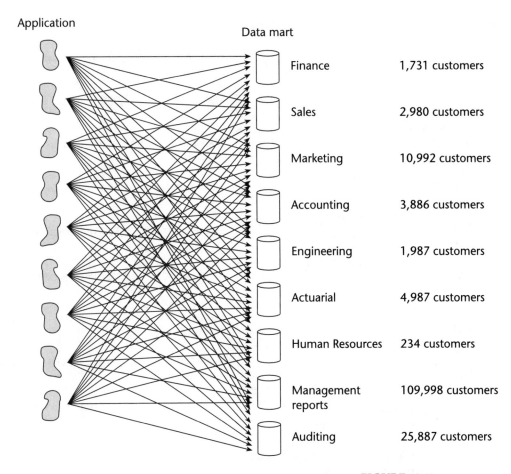

FIGURE 10.12
How many customers are there?

customers can be made, making business sense out of the data becomes a real possibility.

COMBINING THE DATA WAREHOUSE AND THE OPERATIONAL DATA STORE

Another architectural possibility that conflicts with the specifications of the CIF is that of trying to combine the ODS and the data warehouse into the same structure. It is theoretically possible to build such a structure, and under very

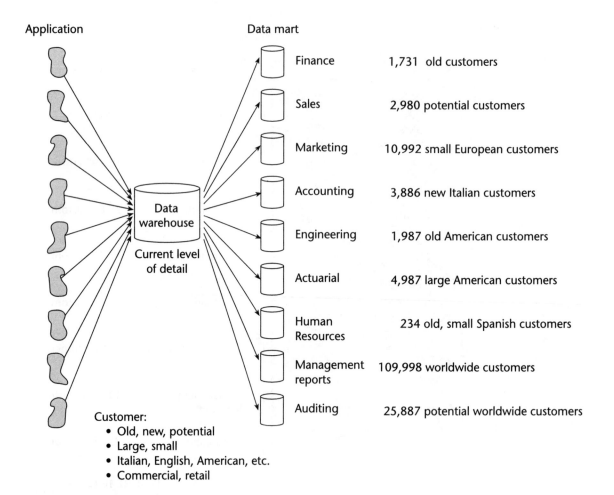

Application

Data mart

Finance	1,731 old customers
Sales	2,980 potential customers
Marketing	10,992 small European customers
Accounting	3,886 new Italian customers
Engineering	1,987 old American customers
Actuarial	4,987 large American customers
Human Resources	234 old, small Spanish customers
Management reports	109,998 worldwide customers
Auditing	25,887 potential worldwide customers

Data warehouse

Current level of detail

Customer:
- Old, new, potential
- Large, small
- Italian, English, American, etc.
- Commercial, retail

FIGURE 10.13

Where there is a single definition of a customer, the different variations can be understood.

limited circumstances, such a combination structure can be made to work.

Where there is a very small amount of data and processing, and an abundance of processing power, it is possible to merge an ODS and a data warehouse into the same structure. The capacity levels for the processor should not exceed more than 5 percent or 10 percent under normal hours of utilization in order for the merger to function properly. Unfortunately, it is not economically feasible to purchase a powerful and versatile machine and use it so

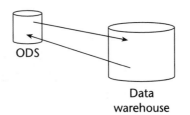

FIGURE 10.14
Another possibility for the CIF is the merging of the ODS and the data warehouse.

sparsely. Figure 10.14 shows the merging of the ODS and the data warehouse into the same structure.

There are many reasons why the ODS and the data warehouse should not be combined. Some of the reasons are very large and important; others are smaller and represent only inconveniences. However, taken together, the reasons all add up to the same thing—the data warehouse and the ODS need to be physically separate entities and environments in order to ensure long-term viability of your information ecosystem.

Combination of Incompatible Transaction Types

Figure 10.15 shows that OLTP and analytical transactions are mixed together when the ODS and the data warehouse are combined.

OLTP transactions and analytical transactions are as different as transaction types can be. When they are separated, many advantageous things happen:

❏ System block sizes can be optimized for one type of transaction or the other.
❏ Buffers can be optimized for one type of processing or the other.
❏ System initialization parameters, such as FREESPACE, can be optimized for one type of activity or the other.
❏ Data can be distributed across system resources (CPU, disk, etc.) for one type of processing or the other.

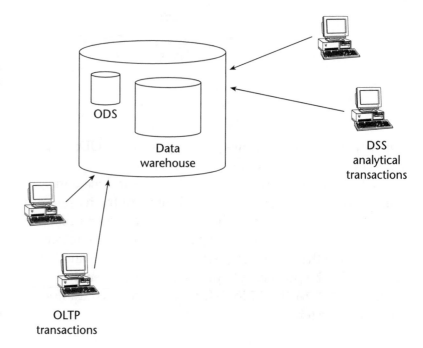

FIGURE 10.15

When the ODS and the data warehouse are combined into the same structure, the types of transactions that are run against the structure are very mixed.

Forced Combination of Incompatible Workload Types

Figure 10.16 shows that there are very different workload patterns for the OLTP environment and the analytical environment.

    The OLTP workload is one where there are peaks and valleys, but where the mean system utilization is a descriptive number. The OLTP workload is one that can be predicted and managed, and the analytical workload is essentially a binary workload. Either the system is being

FIGURE 10.16

When the ODS and the data warehouse are combined into the same structure, the workload that operates against the structure is fundamentally incompatible with itself.

The Operational Workload

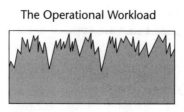

The DSS Workload

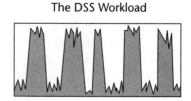

A large processor

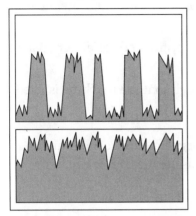

A small processor

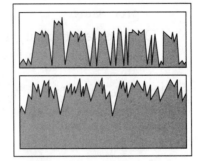

One way to resolve the conflict in the pattern of processing is to buy a mammoth amount of capacity. When you do this:

- The unit price of the hardware is as expensive as it gets.
- You have excess capacity left over.
- The end user is happy with response time.
- The financial manager considers the purchase to be a disaster.

Another way to resolve the conflict presented by mixing incompatible workloads is to buy a small machine and to cram all processing in the small machine. When you do this:

- The machine is used at 100% capacity.
- The end user declares the system unusable.
- The financial manager loves it because it is cheap and the machine is being used at 100%.

FIGURE 10.17
There is no good resolution to the mixing of incompatible workloads.

used heavily or not being used at all. This workload is not predictable and the mean utilization of the system is a useless number in most circumstances. When the ODS and the data warehouse are mixed in the same environment and technology, the two workloads are forced into the same box.

Figure 10.17 shows what happens when the two types of workloads are forced into the same box.

The CIF architect can buy a very large box to try to contain the workload. The problems with a very large configuration of hardware are:

❏ The unit cost of the hardware is expensive. The smaller the configuration, the less expensive the unit of cost.

❏ The hardware cannot be optimized for either style of processing.

❏ The excess capacity is such that the machine is used only 50 percent or less.

In short, the financing of the large box approach to mixing a data warehouse and an ODS is such that it is not very pleasing.

Using a Small Machine to House a Mixed Workload

The alternative approach is to choose a smaller machine and combine the ODS and the data warehouse into the machine. This pleases the finance manager (especially when the finance manager finds out that the machine is being used close to 100 percent of the time). However, there is another set of problems when a small machine is used to contain a mixed workload.

Terrible Response Time   The end user doing OLTP simply is unable to cope with the unpredictable and unacceptable levels of response that are achieved.

Style Incompatibility   The system cannot be tuned or optimized for any style of processing. This workload incompatibility is resolved by separating the ODS and the data warehouse.

Mixing of Communities   When the ODS and the data warehouse are mixed, the DSS analytical community is thrown in with the clerical community. Figure 10.18 illustrates this phenomenon.
Unfortunately, when enough people start to use the combined structure, they start to "step on each other's toes."

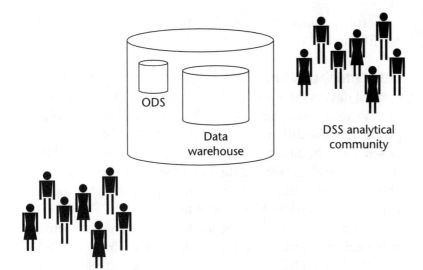

FIGURE 10.18
When the ODS and the data warehouse are combined into the same structure, the different communities they serve are lumped together.

Transmissions Are Incompatible   Figure 10.19 shows that when there is a combined workload, the transmissions across the communications lines are mixed as well.

On the left-hand side of Figure 10.19, the transmission types are not mixed because the ODS and the data warehouse are separated. On the right-hand side, the transmission types are mixed together. In order to achieve a uniform

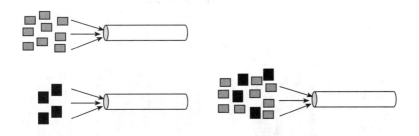

The transmissions when the ODS and the data warehouse are separated.

The transmissions when the ODS and the data warehouse are combined.

FIGURE 10.19
Mixing combined workloads across the communication lines.

and efficient flow, there needs to be a separation of the different transmission types.

Mixed Current and Historical Data   Figure 10.20 shows that ODS current data is mixed with data warehouse historical data.

When current data is mixed with historical data, the problem of the difference in the probability of data access arises. Current data typically has a much higher probability of access than historical data. But when they are mixed together, current data can *hide* behind historical data, making current data hard and inefficient to access.

There is no clear distinction between dynamic summary data and static summary data, as seen in Figure 10.21.

When the ODS and the data warehouse are separated, there is a very real barrier between dynamic summary data and static summary data. When the two are combined, there is the chance that *no* distinction will be made between the two types of summary data. Unfortunately, this blurring of distinctions can cause real confusion.

Overhead of Update   Figure 10.22 shows that when the ODS and the data warehouse are mixed together, every transaction pays the price for overhead of update.

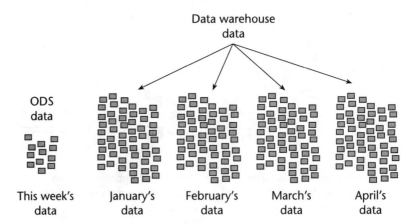

FIGURE 10.20
Current data is mixed with historical data when the ODS is mixed with the data warehouse.

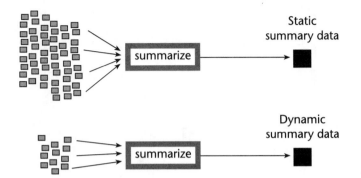

FIGURE 10.21
When the ODS is mixed with the data warehouse, dynamic summary data is mixed with static summary data.

The overhead of update shows up as check pointing, rollback, logging of transactions, and committing data. When update is a possibility, all transactions that are in execution pay the same price of overhead. Even when only one in a thousand transactions actually does update, *all* transactions that are operating pay the price of overhead. When the ODS is separated from the data warehouse, it is very convenient to separate update processing from access processing. Update processing is regularly done in the ODS environment while access-only processing (which is very efficient) is done in the data warehouse environment.

No Optimal Hardware architecture Figure 10.23 shows that when the ODS and the data warehouse are mixed, there is no optimal hardware architecture.

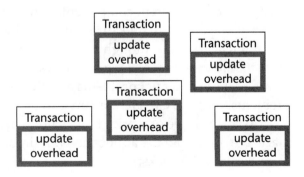

FIGURE 10.22
All transactions pay the price for overhead of update, even when they don't do any update.

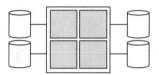

FIGURE 10.23
There is no optimal hardware architecture for the ODS and the data warehouse when they are mixed.

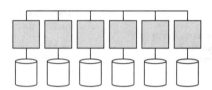

When the ODS is separated from the data warehouse, the ODS operates optimally on an MPP architecture. Depending on the size and the processing done, the data warehouse may or may not run optimally on an MPP architecture. Indeed, the data warehouse may operate optimally on an SMP architecture. When this is the case, the mixing of the two environments causes a dilemma for the CIF architect.

These, then, are the reasons why the ODS and the data warehouse need to be split. They *can* violate the CIF and be combined, but if this is done, the CIF architect needs to be aware that there are prices to be paid.

SUMMARY

The CIF and its different components can be built in many different ways. The architecture suggested by the CIF is not without its variations, though problems can arise when these variations exist. As long as the system architect is aware of these potential problems and the price of these problems, then the CIF architecture can be violated at will.

As an example of a price to be paid, when the data marts are built from the applications environment, there are some severe drawbacks:

❏ The interface between the applications and the data marts turns into a nightmare.

❏ There is no integration foundation.

❏ There is a tremendous amount of redundancy and inconsistent interpretation of data that is necessarily introduced.

As another example of violating the CIF, the ODS and the data warehouse can be built together as a single structure. But when a single structure is created:

❏ OLTP is freely mixed with analytical transactions.

❏ The workload is mixed.

❏ DSS users are mixed with clerical users.

❏ Mixed transmission types are forced into the same communications link.

❏ Current data is mixed with historical data.

This completes our review of an architecture that will embody the information ecosystem of tomorrow's business leaders, the corporate information factory. In the next chapter, we will discuss considerations for building the corporate information factory.

CHAPTER ELEVEN

Building the Corporate Information Factory

Now that we have reviewed the components of the corporate information factory and trade-offs associated with the variations, it is a good time to discuss building it. The information ecosystem that the corporate information factory embodies is very much like any ecosystem in that:

❑ It feeds from a common source of energy, in the form of data, provided by the application environment and external sources.

❑ It transforms this data, through a series of complex processes, into food (i.e., information) consumed by end users of the ecosystem.

❑ It recycles end-user buy-products to further enrich and strengthen the ecosystem.

❑ Its development is *evolutionary in nature.*

In building the corporate information factory, the phrase *"evolutionary in nature"* should be foremost in our minds. This is not to say a *strategic plan* doesn't exist.

Arguably, even the ecosystem in which we live has a strategic plan that provides purpose. However, the development of the corporate information factory should be driven by *strategic actions* aimed at tactical business needs crucial to the survival of the business ecosystem that it supports. With each strategic action—or iteration—the corporate information factory evolves, in form and function, to deliver incremental value to the business. It is only through this iterative delivery that:

❑ Business value is quickly added and relevance is achieved.
❑ Business interest is maintained and heightened.
❑ Details of the strategic plan are materialized.

Through the effective use of a *strategic plan* complemented by *strategic actions*, we can expect to deliver a corporate information factory that evolves to support both the short- and long-term needs of the business.

THE STRATEGIC PLAN

The first step in building the corporate information factory is to understand what competencies drive your business. Business competencies represent areas of proficiency needed to support the business processes (e.g., sales, marketing, service, etc.) as they will exist in tomorrow's business landscape. These competencies are usually composed of a combination of people, processes, and/or systems. Though this may seem like a fairly simple exercise, it is very interesting to note that many existing competencies are being refined, and new competencies are being added, as companies move away from a business model that targets products to the masses, to a model that tailors products to the customer.

In general, the following competencies are common or are becoming common in most companies:

Transaction Management

Product Management

Human Resources Management

Distribution Management

Contact Management

Client Management

Business Intelligence

The next step is to align the different components of the corporate information factory to these core competencies as illustrated in Figure 11.1.

In this example, we see that five competencies have been identified: business intelligence, contact management, product management, human resource (HR) management, and client management. In addition, we can see how these competencies are being positioned to support such business processes as marketing, sales/service, and billing. This overlay of competencies to business processes represents our *business vision*. With that said, let's take a look at how the different components of the corporate information factory align to support this business vision.

Applications Environment

The applications align very nicely to support HR management and client management. In both cases, there appears to be a single, integrated application to support each competency. In contrast, product management consists of three separate product applications with no integration.

Operational Data Store

There appears to be two uses for the operational data store (ODS) in this environment. The first use is as a vehicle to

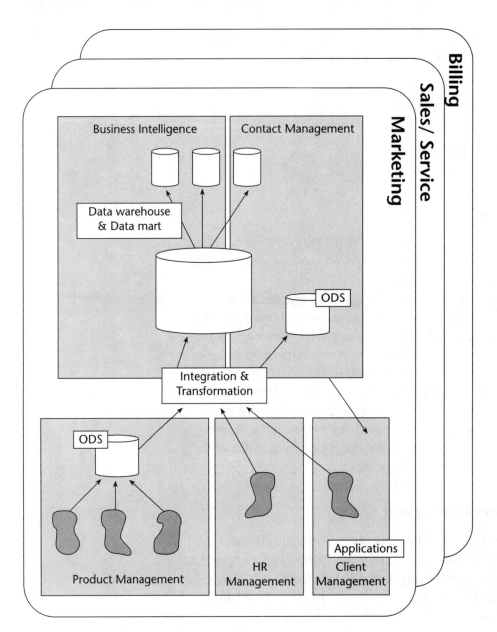

FIGURE 11.1

Aligning the corporate information factory to the core competencies of the business.

provide integration of products within product management. Rather than waiting for this environment to be reengineered, the ODS can be used to expedite delivery of an integrated product view to support immediate business needs. For example, supporting the rollup of customer products into account(s) used in customizing service and billing. In addition, this construct provides a foundation from which reengineering efforts can build.

A second use of the ODS is in support of contact management. In this situation, the ODS provides a consolidated view of application data for use during customer contact activities. In creating this part of the ODS, different contact channels can be assured that their need for customer information will not contend with the needs of the application environment.

Data Warehouse and Data Mart

The data warehouse and data marts seem to be fulfilling two roles. The first role is to deliver integrated data to support business intelligence capabilities. These capabilities support such strategic activities as: profitability analysis, customer profiling, market segmentation, product pricing, and so on.

In addition to these business intelligence capabilities, the data warehouse and data mart are also used to support the lead-generation activities within contact management. It is through these components of the corporate information factory that planning and customer qualification are performed for campaigns and programs. Once a customer is assigned to a campaign(s) and/or program, the ODS is used to provide the operational details necessary to support the dialogue with the customer.

In this strategic plan, the data warehouse and data mart are used to discover and plan business action while the ODS is used to take action.

THE STRATEGIC ACTION

The previous example is by no means definitive, but should give a feel for the process used to derive a high-level strategic plan. It is from this plan that strategic action(s) will be taken.

The first step in determining a strategic action is to select from the business community what competency or competencies should be addressed first. This decision usually follows an assessment in which the high-level needs of each competency area are defined and evaluated. Consider these questions in selecting your competency:

- ❏ What needs are immediate versus long-term? What are the benefits versus risks of meeting or not meeting these needs?
- ❏ How well do the current information systems align to these business needs and the competencies they represent? Are any of the current information systems positioned to support any of these competencies—full or in part? If not, what migration effort must occur?
- ❏ Are any of these needs part of a key corporate initiative?
- ❏ What is the cost to fulfill the need(s)? What funding is available?

Once the competency or competencies have been selected, strategic action can be taken to define the specific capabilities and to deliver/refine the necessary components of the corporate information factory to support these capabilities. Simply put, a capability is a tool that allows the business community to derive value out of the corporate information factory in support of a selected business competency. For example, a popular business intelligence capability would be one that supports profitability analysis. In addition, the necessary organization, technology, and procedures are employed to support administration and ongoing development.

DEVELOPMENT LIFE CYCLES

There are many stark differences between the different components of the CIF. Perhaps the greatest difference is the development life cycle used to implement the capabilities. Figure 11.2 outlines the different development life cycles found in the CIF.

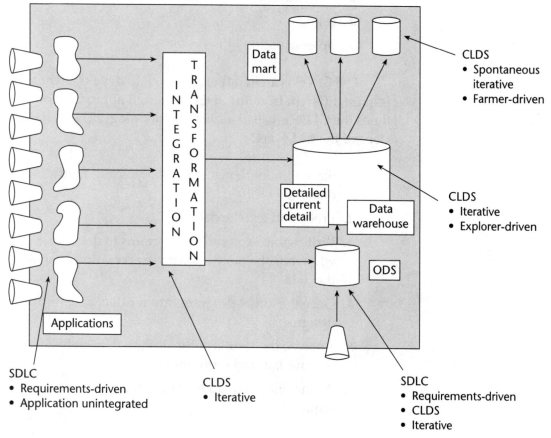

FIGURE 11.2

The different development life cycles found throughout the CIF.

There are two basic types of development life cycles—the systems development life cycle SDLC and the CLDS. The CLDS is in many ways the reverse image of the SDLC. The SDLC is often called a *waterfall* methodology because one phase feeds into the other. The classical stages of the SDLC are:

❑ Requirements gathering

❑ Analysis

❑ Design

❑ Programming

❑ Testing

❑ Implementation

The CLDS is an iterative approach to development and is quite different from the SDLC waterfall approach. Sometimes the CLDS is called a *spiral* methodology. The classical steps of the CLDS are:

1. Start with implemented data, typically transaction data.

2. Probe and test the data.

3. Write some exploratory programs to determine what must be done in order to access and analyze the data.

4. Once the initial programs are written, do a formal design.

5. Analyze the results of the design, then go back and reformulate and reprogram.

6. As the final step, understand what the requirements are.

The SDLC is typically found in the applications arena. Because of the constant change that is endemic to the I & T

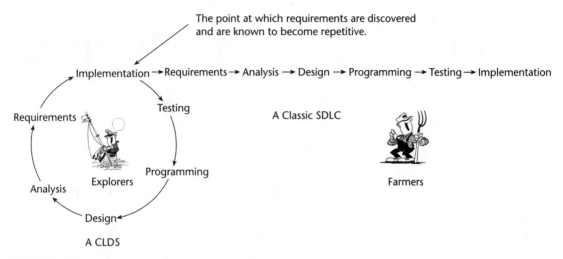

The point at which requirements are discovered and are known to become repetitive.

Implementation → Requirements → Analysis → Design → Programming → Testing → Implementation

A Classic SDLC

A CLDS

Farmers

FIGURE 11.3

There is an important relationship between the SDLC and the CLDS.

layer, the CLDS approach works best with the programs that must be developed there.

The ODS contains elements of both the SDLC and the CLDS. Because of this confusion, the ODS is the most difficult structure in the CIF to build successfully.

CLDS can apply to both the data warehouse and the data mart. However, there is a variation to the development life cycle on the data mart when in use by a farmer. The data warehouse is generally used by explorers. As a result, CLDS methodology proves to be very effective. In contrast, farmer activities are more repetitive and predictable. In this environment, the SDLC may prove to be more appropriate. Figure 11.3 makes the distinction between different kinds of development life cycles.

MANAGING DIFFERENT ORGANIZATIONAL UNITS

Not surprisingly, there are different kinds of organizational units found scattered across the CIF. Figure 11.4 shows

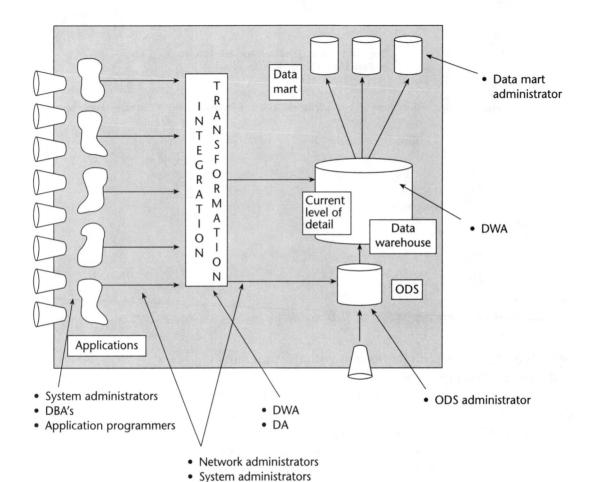

FIGURE 11.4

The organizational roles of different groups.

some of the more important organizational roles and where they are found.

System administrators are found in the management of the applications arena and in the administration of the network. Database administrators (DBAs) are found in the applications arena as well as applications programmers. Network administrators are found in the network management environment. Data warehouse administrators (DWAs) are located in the specification of the I & T layer and the data warehouse venue. The data administrator is involved with the I & T layer. The ODS requires its own administrator. Finally, the data mart is under the guidance of the departments that own the data mart itself with its own set of administrators and management.

DEPLOYING DATABASES

There are any number of strategies for the deployment of database management systems across the components of the CIF. The first strategy is on a *niche* basis, where different DBMS are used for different components based on an ideal fit. In Figure 11.5, there is a different DBMS

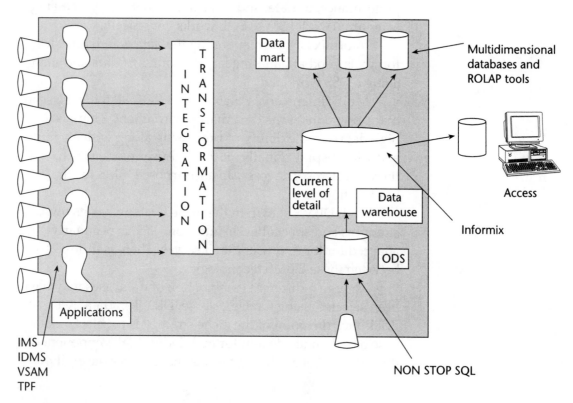

FIGURE 11.5

DBMS uniquely suited for their niches—one approach toward DBMS and the CIF.

for every part of the CIF. For the applications arena, there are:

> IMS
>
> IDMS
>
> VSAM
>
> TPF

These DBMS are good at moving transactions and doing repetitive transactions. They can yield high performance and a very high degree of availability.

At the ODS is Tandem's NON STOP SQL. For mixed-mode processing, where a combination of high performance, update, and some amount of DSS processing is required, NON STOP SQL works very nicely.

Informix is shown operating the data warehouse. Informix is good at handling large amounts of data and managing a DSS workload.

Multidimensional database and ROLAP tools are seen managing data at the data mart environment. There is a high degree of flexibility of processing along with elegant end-user display. Finally, at the end-user workstation, there is Microsoft Access, an all-purpose DBMS for the workstation.

Each DBMS shown in the niche strategy has its own strengths and specialties. In addition, each is peculiarly adapted for the end user that it serves. There is little overlap between these DBMS technologies.

Though a different combination of databases may have been selected using Oracle, Sybase, DB2, Teradata, Red Brick, etc., the point of the niche strategy is to select a database based on its ideal fit for each individual component of the CIF. The niche strategy is one that evolves naturally.

The General-purpose DBMS Strategy

There are other strategies besides the niche strategy. Another is the *general-purpose* strategy. In Figure 11.6, the same DBMS—is found in more than one component of the CIF. At first glance, this appears to be a contradiction of the niche strategy. But upon a closer look, the general-purpose strategy ends up looking very similar to the niche strategy.

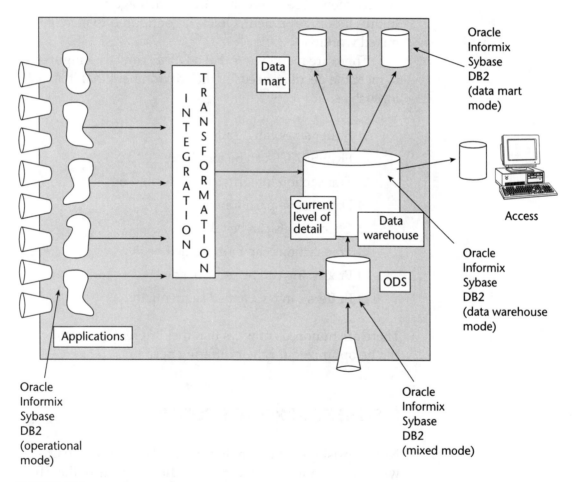

FIGURE 11.6
The same DBMS can be used in different modes.

The reason why the general-purpose strategy looks a lot like the niche strategy is because even though the same DBMS is used in multiple places, the DBMS is configured very differently in different components. In other words, it may be Oracle in the applications arena and Oracle in the data warehouse, but the way that Oracle is configured in one place is not at all the way Oracle is configured elsewhere. In the applications environment, Oracle is configured for running transactions. In the data warehouse environment, Oracle is configured to manage a lot of data. In the ODS environment, Oracle is configured to manage a mixed workload.

There are many ways that a DBMS can be configured to meet the peculiar needs of the environment that it is cast in, such as:

❑ Buffer sizes can be altered.
❑ FREESPACE can be modified.
❑ Transaction integrity can be turned off.
❑ Data can be partitioned.
❑ Checkpoints can be taken.
❑ Transactions can be governed.
❑ Processing can be prioritized.
❑ Buffers can be scanned sequentially.

There are hundreds of ways that the different environments can be optimized for their differing needs.

DIFFERENT HARDWARE PLATFORMS

Not surprisingly, different hardware platforms and hardware architectures work better in different parts of the CIF. Three types of hardware architectures, shown in Figure 11.7, are:

1. Parallel MPP architectures: Multiple units of data are tied together by a common "backbone."

2. Parallel SMP architectures: Multiple processors are tied together in a shared memory configuration.

3. Uniprocessor architectures: A single storage device is controlled by a single processor, much as in a workstation or a mainframe processor.

The applications environment uses a parallel SMP architecture well; for smaller amounts of processing, a uniprocessor architecture is sufficient. The ODS environ-

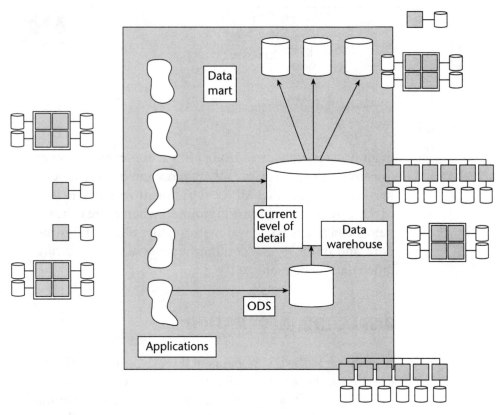

FIGURE 11.7
Different hardware architectures have a different affinity with the various components of the CIF.

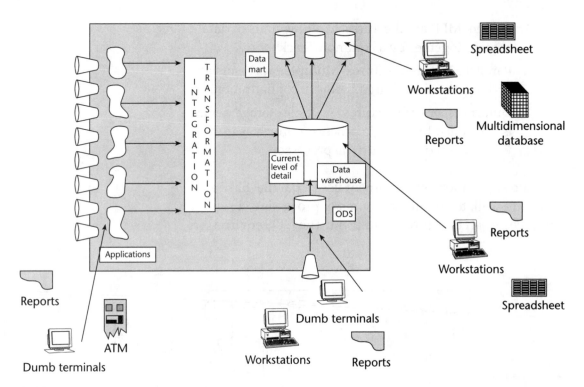

FIGURE 11.8
The different forms of display at the different components.

ment has a particularly strong affinity for an MPP processing environment. The data warehouse environment operates well on a parallel MPP environment when there is a lot of data and on an SMP configuration when there is less data. Data marts work well with smaller SMP configurations and uniprocessor configurations where there is not much data to be managed.

DISPLAYING INFORMATION

In addition to the components of the CIF needing different DBMSs (or the same DBMS configured in very different ways) and hardware platforms, there is the need for multiple kinds of displays of information. Figure 11.8 shows that information is displayed in a different mode throughout the CIF.

At the applications level, data is displayed using reports, dumb terminals, and on direct consumer interaction devices, such as an ATM. The ODS uses workstations, dumb terminals, and reports for the display of its information. The data warehouse has a wide variety of displays, such as workstations, spreadsheets, and reports. The data marts have the same display mechanisms as the data warehouse, including multidimensional DBMS.

The mode that information is displayed suits the style of processing. Where there is repetitive processing that is occurring, such as at the applications level, a dumb terminal suffices. With free-form, analytical processing, where iterative analysis is being done, powerful and flexible displays are in order.

SUMMARY

The process of building the corporate information factory begins with defining the strategic plan and selecting the first business competency to develop. From here, strategic actions are taken and valued business capabilities are delivered.

There is a different development life cycle that applies across the CIF to deliver capabilities. The classical SDLC is used in the applications and the ODS arena, and the reverse of the SDLC—the CLDS—is found in the data mart and the data warehouse environment. The explorer development life cycle—the CLDS—turns into the farmer's development life cycle—the SDLC—when the requirements of processing are discovered.

There are two strategies for deploying databases within the corporate information factory. On a niche basis, a variety of specialized databases can be used to optimize performance within each component of the corporate information factory. Alternatively, general-purpose databases can be tuned according to the varied processing demands of each component offering near-optimal performance.

Different hardware architectures support components of the CIF. MPP hardware environments fit very well with the ODS and occasionally with the data warehouse. SMP and uniprocessor architectures fit nicely with the data warehouse and the data mart environment.

In this chapter, we discussed people, process techniques, and technology considerations in building the corporate information factory. In the next chapter, we review the key considerations in managing the corporate information factory.

12

Managing the Corporate Information Factory

Once the CIF is built—in whole or in part—it requires ongoing systems management. Because of the diversity of processing that occurs within the CIF, it is no surprise that there are many different types of systems management tools that are needed to monitor and run day-to-day operations. The CIF is simply much too big and much too diverse for any one suite of systems management tools to suffice. Indeed, the parameters of importance from one component of the CIF to another are so different that no one approach to systems management can be undertaken. Instead, the needs for systems management must be considered on a component-by-component basis (Figure 12.1):

❑ In the applications environment, systems management needs are characterized by transaction response time and availability.

❑ In the I & T layer, systems management needs are characterized by the ability to handle complexity, and the ability to gracefully and efficiently orches-

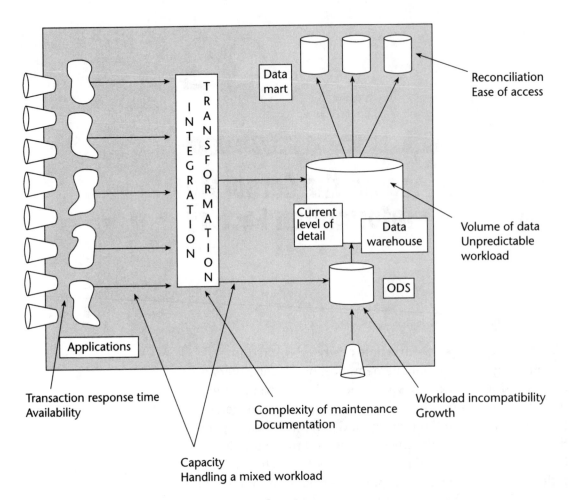

Reconciliation
Ease of access

Volume of data
Unpredictable
workload

ODS

Applications

Transaction response time
Availability

Complexity of maintenance
Documentation

Workload incompatibility
Growth

Capacity
Handling a mixed workload

FIGURE 12.1

The characterization of systems management needs within the CIF.

trate maintenance with an ever-changing set of requirements.

❏ In the ODS environment, systems management needs are characterized by workload incompatibility and growth. As discussed earlier, this could easily become the most complex systems management task of all.

❏ In the data warehouse, systems management needs are characterized by volumes of data and unpredictable workload.

❏ In the data mart environment, systems management needs are characterized by reconciliation of data, and ease of access and manipulation.

❏ In the Internet and intranet, systems management needs are characterized by network capacity and the ability to handle a mixed transmission workload.

Each of these issues of ongoing management will be addressed, component by component.

ONGOING MANAGEMENT—APPLICATIONS

The primary issue of ongoing systems management for the applications arena is that of online response time and online systems availability. If the online system is not up and running, and if online response time is not adequate, then the end user considers the application systems a failure. The desired response time is in the one- to two-second range. The systems availability desired is seven days a week, 24 hours a day—7×24.

There are many ways to obtain such a high degree of availability and responsiveness. The simplest way is to supply the applications environment with ample hardware resources. The problem with managing performance with resources is that it is very expensive and that, for some problems, additional systems resources do not improve performance or availability. Sometimes performance and availability are constrained by the software that uses the hardware. For example, let's say that you decide to upgrade your hardware environment from one CPU to two CPUs in an effort to improve transaction performance. It is possible that you may not realize any performance gain if the DBMS (i.e., software) is not designed to distribute data and processing across multiple CPUs. Your only hope at this point would be to upgrade to a faster CPU or buy a new database.

A better long-term approach is to monitor the environment closely. With an OLTP monitor, two results can be achieved:

1. "Hot spots" and trouble areas can be identified and corrected before they become a major problem. Corrections could consist of simple software changes, or indexing and redistribution of data.

2. Capacity can be watched so that as soon as a legitimate need for more capacity arises, additional hardware can be procured.

Another approach to the optimization of the response time is to design applications so that optimal response time can be achieved. In this approach, called the *standard work unit* approach, programs are written so that each uses a small and uniform amount of resources. Thus, the transactions that are created run through the system at a very efficient rate.

Another consideration of ongoing success of the applications environment is that of placing the applications environment on the appropriate technology. Indeed, all CIF components need to be placed on top of technology that is optimal for their execution.

ONGOING MANAGEMENT—INTEGRATION AND TRANSFORMATION LAYER

Daily operations do not occur in the I & T layer in the same sense that they do in the applications environment or in other environments. Yet the I & T layer needs to be managed just like any other component of the CIF. The following things are vital to the ongoing management of this layer:

❑ The maintenance of the code created for the I & T layer

❑ The efficiency of execution of the code inside the I & T layer

❑ The creation of metadata as a by-product of code inside the I & T layer

❑ The creation of process and procedures to audit the I & T layer

The programs and processes within the I & T layer are notoriously dynamic because they sit in the crossroads between the applications environment and the data integration mechanisms of the CIF—the data warehouse and ODS. As a result, the I & T layer has the potential to change when:

❑ The application environment changes

❑ The data warehouse changes

❑ The operational data store changes

To further complicate matters, the nature of data warehouse development is very iterative. As a result, changes occur frequently. As you can see, the I & T layer is subject to frequent change and, therefore, requires constant attention and maintenance.

Creating and Maintaining the Interface

One of the most effective approaches to managing the I & T layer is to use a tool of automation for the creation and maintenance of the interface. Instead of having manual programming as the basis for the creation of the I & T code, a tool of automation creates code for the interface automatically. This means that code is created and maintained much more quickly and cost-effectively.

Executing the Code

The efficiency of the execution of the code in the I & T layer is another ongoing challenge. There can be some gains in performance by carefully designing the programs and processes to effectively execute in the targeted hardware and DBMS environment. In addition, significant performance improvement can be realized by altering the means by which application *change* transactions are captured. Rather than sifting through the DBMS or DBMS backup file, the DBMS *log* can be used to capture application change transactions far more efficiently. The trade-off is that programs that read the log file tend to be fairly complex given the challenges involved in interpreting it. When log tapes are used as a source for refreshment:

❑ Only the data that has been added, changed, or deleted is considered for refreshment. There is no need to pass massive amounts of data in the applications database looking for data that might be a candidate for refreshment.

❑ The log tape can be passed offline, not requiring the native DBMS to be up and active.

❑ The machine the log tape runs on can be a small machine where the cost of processing is not an issue. When the native DBMS must be read, the reading inevitably takes place on a large machine whose cost of processing is very high.

❑ Contention for resources with the operational systems are minimized.

The Production of Metadata

While a powerful argument can be made for the usage of a tool of automation for productivity and maintenance, an even more powerful case can be made when it comes to the production of metadata as a by-product of creating code. When using a tool of automation to build the I & T layer, metadata about the processing is produced as a by-product of the creation of code. The programmer thinks that he or she is creating code that defines the interface between an application file and a data warehouse file when, in fact, that is exactly what the programmer is doing. After the programmer has finished the creation of the code, the tool of automation simultaneously produces relevant metadata.

When a tool of automation is used to create and maintain the I & T layer and metadata is produced as a by-product, then:

❏ The production of metadata is automatic, requiring no extra effort by the programmer.

❏ The metadata is produced for every new iteration of development, thereby keeping a complete historical version of the metadata applicable to the data in the warehouse.

❏ The metadata mappings are produced completely, so that there are no incomplete gaps in the metadata.

❏ No extra cost justification effort is required for the production of the metadata.

❏ The logic of transformation can be included as part of metadata.

❏ Standard business rules can be managed and reused.

ONGOING MANAGEMENT—OPERATIONAL DATA STORE

The ODS is easily the most complex and difficult arena for ongoing systems management because it is truly a mixed environment. There are elements of OLTP, DSS/informational, and every other kind of processing in the ODS. This results in an environment that supports high availability, one- to two-second transaction response time, and complex DSS queries. Because of this mixture, managing the ODS environment is difficult, even under the best of circumstances.

The only real way the ODS environment can be managed is to slice the ODS day into different segments and manage each segment differently from the others. At 10:00 A.M., the ODS is an OLTP. At 5:30 P.M., the ODS is a batch environment. At 2:45 A.M., the ODS is a DSS machine.

Because the ODS is in fact the same physical entity and the work that is done is only superficially governed by the time of day that processing is done, the ODS ends up not being optimal for anything. At best, the ODS is *acceptable* for all the roles it plays.

Some of the tools and approaches used to manage the ODS environment on an ongoing basis include:

❑ Monitoring the ODS using an OLTP monitor
❑ Monitoring the ODS using a DSS activity monitor
❑ Monitoring the ODS using a data monitor

Another approach is to use hardware, optimal to the ODS environment. The ODS operates well on an MPP environment given the fault tolerance inherent to the hardware redundancy of the architecture. Also, because CPU resources are not shared in this environment (memory and disk) and operational transactions are relatively predictive, the database design can generally be tuned to optimize performance by minimizing or eliminating resource contention.

Another technique to ensure the best overall performance of the ODS is to frequently purge or move to the data warehouse from the ODS environment. Data that sits around the ODS and has a low probability of access is anathema to the efficient running of the environment.

ONGOING MANAGEMENT—DATE WAREHOUSE

The primary issue of ongoing data warehouse success is the management of the volume of data that arises in it. Truly magnanimous amounts of data tend to accumulate in the data warehouse. In response, the DWA needs to make sure that the volumes of data that reside in the data warehouse belong there.

The way that the DWA ensures that no dormant data creeps into the data warehouse is to employ a data warehouse usage monitor. This monitor tracks very closely who uses what data in the data warehouse. By understanding what data has been used, the DWA is able to understand what data has not been used so that steps can be taken to archive or delete it. In addition, the DWA can employ this usage information to tune the data warehouse through indexing, partitioning or summarization of data.

The second aspect of data warehousing that needs to be managed over time is that of the quality of data within the data warehouse in terms of completeness and accuracy. As time passes, it is inevitable that data of inferior quality creeps into the data warehouse. The DWA has the task of identifying and correcting the data that is incorrect in the data warehouse.

ONGOING MANAGEMENT—DATA MART

In many ways, the data mart is the easiest of the environments to manage over time because:

❏ It is a relatively small environment, in terms of data.

❏ It is a self-contained environment.

❏ It is relevant to only one department.

❏ Data is already scrubbed and integrated upon arriving at the data mart.

❏ The hardware and software found in the data mart environment are amenable to change.

The challenges related to the administration of the data mart environment over time are:

❏ Metadata infrastructure

   ❏ The building of the infrastructure

   ❏ The maintenance of the infrastructure

   ❏ The compatibility of the infrastructure with the tools found in the environment

❏ Capacity planning as data volumes and end-user community grows

❏ Performance tuning as end-user demands grow

ONGOING MANAGEMENT—INTERNET AND INTRANET

The two most pressing issues of network management for the CIF over time are those of network capacity and the ability to handle a mixed transmission workload. As time passes, the volume of data passed into the CIF and throughout the CIF grows. The configuration that is adequate one year will most likely be inadequate the next.

Another problem is that of an ever-increasing mixed workload. As long as the workload is small, predictable, and homogeneous, the line used to handle the transmissions is not a big issue. In contrast, as the demands on volume grow and as the workload passed over the line grows in diversity, the selection of the line becomes a major issue.

MONITORING THE CORPORATE INFORMATION FACTORY

Because of the diversity of processing and the wide disparity in the parameters of success found in the CIF, it should come as no surprise that different kinds of monitors are required for the management of the CIF (Figure 12.2).

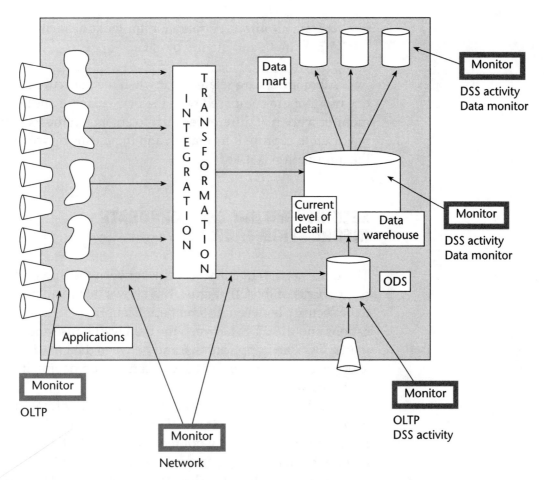

FIGURE 12.2
The different kinds of monitors that are needed for the management of the CIF.

The figure shows that there are the following monitors:

❏ **OLTP monitors.** OLTP monitors are designed to manage transaction response time.

❏ **DSS monitors.** DSS activity monitors look at system activity from the standpoint of DSS activity, not OLTP activity. Among other things, a DSS monitor can help identify dormant data inside a data warehouse.

❏ **Network monitors.** Similar to OLTP monitors, network monitors keep track of general network activity.

❑ **Data monitors.** A data monitor looks at such things as growth and quality of data.

All monitors are related. But when the particulars of one monitor are compared with the particulars of another monitor, very real differences start to emerge in the technology used to capture information and the means by which the information is used.

SECURITY WITHIN THE CORPORATE INFORMATION FACTORY

There is a need to manage security between the different components of the CIF. Figure 12.3 shows that there needs to be security between different applications, between applications and the ODS, between the data warehouse and data marts, ODS, and applications, and between data marts. In short, every component of the CIF can end up having its own security.

The levels of security that are required vary for each component and each instance of each component. For example, some data marts may not require any security while other data marts require great security. Some applications may require simple logon/logoff security, while other applications require DBMS-based security.

The different security needs across the CIF can be divided into different levels of classifications:

❑ 1%—very high levels of security

❑ 5%—high levels of security

❑ 25%—some levels of security

❑ 74%—little or no security

These levels show that only a small fraction of the data in the CIF needs a truly high degree of security. At the other

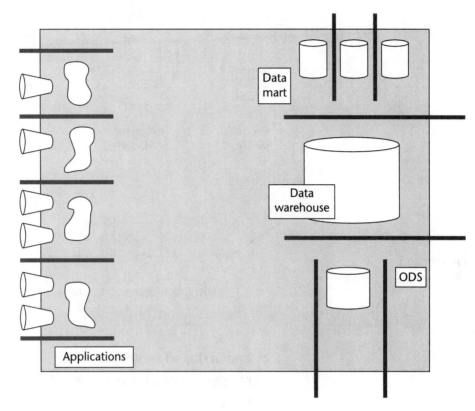

Data mart

Data warehouse

ODS

Applications

FIGURE 12.3
Security in the CIF is first sectioned off by component.

end of the spectrum, most data needs little or no security. The way that different levels of security are implemented is through different technological approaches. Each of the approaches depicted in Figure 12.4 has its unique advantages and disadvantages:

1. Firewall security.
   - ❏ Easy to construct
   - ❏ Cheap
   - ❏ Does not protect data as it passes along the network, either entering or leaving the database
   - ❏ No protection offered when firewall has been breached

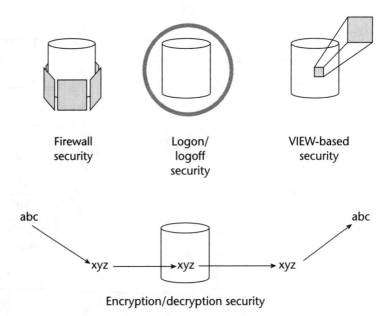

FIGURE 12.4
There are different levels of security.

2. Logon/logoff security.
   ❏ Often comes with software
   ❏ Easy to implement
   ❏ Cheap
   ❏ Does not protect data as it passes along the network, either entering or leaving the database
   ❏ No protection offered when logon/logoff has been breached
3. VIEW-based DBMS security.
   ❏ Comes with DBMS software
   ❏ Cumbersome to implement, manage
   ❏ Cheap
   ❏ Does not protect data as it passes along the network, either entering or leaving the database
   ❏ No protection offered when VIEW has been breached

4. Encryption/decryption.
   ❑ Relatively expensive
   ❑ Not necessarily difficult to implement
   ❑ Does not allow data to be accessed for general-purpose processing
   ❑ Protects data as it passes along the network, either entering or leaving the database
   ❑ Protection offered when firewall, logon/logoff, and/or VIEW have been breached

The different types of security have different levels of effectiveness and costs. In general, the less effective the type of security, the less it costs and the fewer the restrictions that accompany the technique. Conversely, the greater the level of security, the greater the cost and the more restrictions that accompany the technique. The different approaches to security can be used alone or in combination with each other.

ARCHIVAL PROCESSING

This is a key aspect of systems management in a maturing information ecosystem. While there is a steady and predictable flow of data throughout the CIF and while data resides in the data warehouse for lengthy periods of time, there nevertheless is a need for archival processing to ensure optimal use of resources and recoverability of the corporate information factory. Figure 12.5 shows that data is archived from the different components of the corporate information factory. Each instance of archival has its own unique set of considerations.

Applications Archiving

One reason for applications archival processing is transaction-recovery backup. Periodically—typically daily—data is

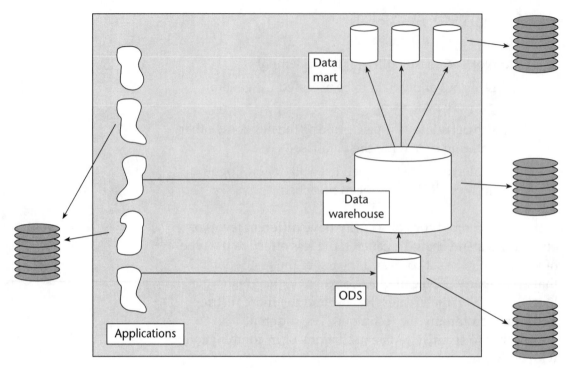

FIGURE 12.5
*Data is periodically archived
onto sequential forms of
storage.*

removed from the applications log or journal tape and is
placed onto an archive log. The transaction archive log is
used for recovery of an online database in the case of a failure where full backup and recovery must be done.

The second case for applications archival is to provide
a location and vehicle for detailed transaction adjustments.
When accounting activity is done in the applications environment, it may be necessary to keep a long-standing record
of the activities that occurred there. If such a record is necessary, then an archival log must be kept. In any case, when
the archival log is kept at the applications level, the age of
the data is minimal. The data is rarely more than a month
old inside the archives themselves.

Operational Data Store Archiving

Nearly all data that ages in the ODS passes to the data warehouse. Therefore, it is unusual to have an archiving facility in the ODS environment. On those rare occasions where there is an archiving facility in the ODS environment, it is because some summary data has been created. Since the ODS contains dynamic summary data only, it may make sense to keep an archival log of what the dynamic summary values were as created. Such a log can serve many purposes. One such purpose is as backup to the information that was available to a crucial decision.

Data Warehouse Archiving

The very essence of the data warehouse is archival data. For this reason it may seem strange that the data warehouse itself should occasionally have its own data archived. However, as the volume of data in the data warehouse grows and as the probability of the usage of that data decreases, the data in the data warehouse needs to be archived. Of course, if the probability of data usage truly goes to zero, then the data should be removed, not archived. However, once data has gone through the process of systematization and integration, the cost of reconstructing the data if it should ever be needed again is such that nearly all data in the data warehouse should be archived, not purged.

Data Mart Archiving

The data marts, like the data warehouse, need to be archived occasionally. In the case of the data marts, data that is the most granular is purged the quickest. The higher the degree of summarization, the less likely a unit of data is to be purged from the data mart environment.

Another important factor relating to the archiving of information from the data mart environment is that this environment does not grow to the size of the data warehouse. Because of this difference in size, the archiving of data from the data mart is done much less frequently and much less rigorously than the archiving that is done in the data warehouse environment.

Archiving Medium

The archiving is done to a medium that can hold bulk amounts of data, but where the electronic image and substance of the record can be maintained. The usual case is for the retrieval of the first archival record to take as much as a minute and the access of subsequent records to occur at regular electronic speeds.

A standard storage medium for archival storage is siloed storage. It can store electronic images very inexpensively and provide quick access once the first record is retrieved.

Another consideration of archival processing is that of the reliability and longevity of the medium itself. It goes without saying that any medium used for archiving must be able to physically store the data for long periods of time with a very low rate of corruption.

SUMMARY

Because of the very large differences in content, operation, and processing among the components of the CIF, the ongoing issues of maintenance and operation are likewise very different.

Different kinds of monitors are used to capture key content information within each component of the corporate information factory. This information is used to support such management activities as capacity planning, performance tuning, and quality control.

Managing security is an important aspect of the CIF; in general, security is accomplished on a component-by-component basis. There are different levels of security that can be applied in different places. The greater the degree of security, the more the cost and the restrictions of the security. Different types of security can be used in conjunction with each other.

One of the essential systems management activities within the CIF is the occasional archiving of the data.

IN CLOSING

Well, it is time to set sail on the sea of information and the destination is clear. Today's business is quickly redefining itself from one where products are targeted to the masses to one where products are tailored to the customer. Unfortunately, today's information systems were not designed for targeting products to the masses. What is needed is a comprehensive and adaptive information solution that can leverage these systems to quickly deliver on the evolving needs of the business. This solution must be able to quickly exploit best-of-breed technologies as they become available. Additionally, this solution must promote an iterative delivery strategy that evolves the information ecosystem while demonstrating incremental value to the business. The corporate information factory presented in these pages is such a solution that has proven itself over time.

We hope that this book has helped you understand the potential and promise of the corporate information factory in supporting the evolving information needs of your business. Additionally, we hope this book will help you charter your course in its use and evolution.

Bon voyage!

Glossary

access the operation of seeking, reading, or writing data on a storage unit.

access method a technique used to transfer a physical record from or to a mass storage device.

access mode a technique in which a specific logical record is obtained from or placed onto a file assigned to a mass storage device.

access pattern the general sequence by which the data structure is accessed (e.g., from tuple to tuple, from record to record, from segment to segment, etc.).

access plan the control structure produced during program preparation and used by a Database Manager to process SQL statements during application execution.

access time the time interval between the instant an instruction initiates a request for data and the instant the first of the data satisfying the request is delivered. Note that there is a difference—sometimes large—between the time data is first delivered and the time when *all* the data is delivered.

accuracy a qualitative assessment of freedom from error or a quantitative measure of the magnitude of error, expressed as a function of relative error.

active data dictionary a data dictionary that is the sole source for an application program insofar as metadata is concerned.

activity (1) the lowest-level function on an activity chart (sometimes called the "atomic level"); (2) a logical description of a function performed by an enterprise; (3) a procedure (automated or not) designed for the fulfillment of an activity.

activity ratio the fraction of records in a database which have activity or are otherwise accessed in a given period of time or in a given batch run.

ad hoc processing one time only, casual access and manipulation of data on parameters never before used.

address an identification (e.g., number, name, storage location, byte offset, etc.) for a location where data is stored.

addressing the means of assigning data to storage locations and locating the data upon subsequent retrieval, on the basis of the key of the data.

after image the snapshot of data placed on a log upon the completion of a transaction.

agent of change a motivating force large enough not to be denied—usually aging of systems, changes in technology, radical changes in requirements, etc.

AIX Advanced Interactive eXecutive—IBM's version of the UNIX operating system.

algorithm a set of statements organized to solve a problem in a finite number of steps.

alias an alternative label used to refer to a data element.

alphabetic a representation of data using letters—upper- and/or lowercase—only.

alphanumeric a representation of data using numbers and/or letters and punctuation.

analytical processing the usage of the computer to produce an analysis for management decision, usually involving trend analysis, drill-down analysis, demographic analysis, profiling, etc.

ANSI American National Standards Institute.

anticipatory staging the technique of moving blocks of data from one storage device to another with a shorter access time, in anticipation of their being needed by a program in execution or a program soon to go into execution.

API (Application Program Interface) the common set of parameters needed to connect the communications between programs.

application a group of algorithms and data interlinked to support an organizational requirement.

application blocking of data the grouping into the same physical unit of storage multiple occurrences of data controlled at the application level.

application database a collection of data organized to support a specific application.

archival database a collection of data of an historical nature. As a rule, archival data cannot be updated. Each unit of archival data is related to a moment in time, now passed.

area in network databases, a named collection of records that can contain occurrences of one or more record types. A record type can occur in more than one area.

artifact a design technique used to represent referential integrity in the DSS environment.

artificial intelligence the capability of a system to perform functions typically associated with human intelligence and reasoning.

association a relationship between two entities that is represented in a data model.

associative storage (1) a storage device whose records are identified by a specific part of their contents rather than their name or physical position in the database; (2) content-addressable memory. *See also* **parallel search storage.**

atomic (1) data stored in a data warehouse; (2) the lowest level of process analysis.

atomic database a database made up of primarily atomic data; a data warehouse; a DSS foundation database.

atomicity the property where a group of actions is invisible to other actions executing concurrently; yielding the effect of serial execution. It is recoverable with successful completion (i.e., commit) or total backout (i.e., rollback) of previous changes associated with that group.

atomic level data data with the lowest level of granularity. Atomic level data sits in a data warehouse and is time-variant (i.e., accurate as of some moment in time now passed).

attribute a property that can assume values for entities or relationships. Entities can be assigned several attributes (e.g., a tuple in a relationship consists of values). Some systems also allow relationships to have attributes as well.

audit trail data that is available to trace activity, usually update activity.

authorization identifier a character string that designates a set of privilege descriptors.

availability a measure of the reliability of a system, indicating the fraction of time the system is up and available divided by the amount of time the system should be up and available. Note that there is a difference between a piece of hardware being available and the systems running on that hardware also being available.

backend processor a database machine or an intelligent disk controller.

back up to restore the database to its state at some previous moment in time.

backup a file serving as a basis for backing up a database. Usually a snapshot of a database at some previous moment in time.

Backus-Naur Form (BNF) a metalanguage used to specify or describe the syntax of a language. In BNF, each symbol on the left side of the forms can be replaced by the symbol strings on the right side of the forms to develop sentences in the grammar of the defined language. Synonymous with Backus—Normal Form.

backward recovery a recovery technique that restores a database to an earlier state by applying previous images.

base relation a relation that is not derivable from other relations in the database.

batch computer environment in which programs (usually long running, sequentially oriented) access data exclusively, and user interaction is not allowed while the activity is occurring.

batch environment a sequentially dominated mode of processing; in batch, input is collected and stored for later processing. Once collected, the batch input is transacted sequentially against one or more databases.

batch window the time at which the online system is available for batch or sequential processing. The batch window occurs during nonpeak processing hours.

before image a snapshot of a record prior to update, usually placed on an activity log.

bill of materials a listing of the parts used in a manufacturing process along with the relation of one part to another insofar as assembly of the final product is concerned. The bill of materials is a classical recursive structure.

binary element a constituent element of data that exists as either of two values or states—either true or false, or one or zero.

binary search a dichotomizing search with steps where the sets of remaining items are partitioned into two equal parts.

bind (1) to assign a value to a data element, variable, or parameter; (2) the attachment of a data definition to a program prior to the execution of the program.

binding time the moment when the data description known to the dictionary is assigned to or bound to the procedural code.

bit—(b)inary digi(t) the lowest level of storage. A bit can be in a 1 state or a 0 state.

bit map a specialized form of an index indicating the existence or nonexistence of a condition for a group of blocks or records. Bit maps are expensive to build and maintain, but provide very fast comparison and access facilities.

block (1) a basic unit of structuring storage; (2) the physical unit of transport and storage. A block usually contains one or more records (or contains the space for one or more records). In some DBMS, a block is called a page.

blocking combining of two or more physical records so that they are physically colocated together. The result of their physical colocation is that the records can be accessed and fetched by execution of a single machine instruction.

block splitting the data management activity where data in a filled block is written into two unfilled blocks, leaving space for future insertions and updates in the two partially filled blocks.

B-tree a binary storage structure and access method that maintains order in a database by continually dividing possible choices into two equal parts and reestablishing pointers to the respective sets, while not allowing more than two levels of difference to exist concurrently.

buffer an area of storage that holds data temporarily in main memory while data is being transmitted, received, read, or written. A buffer is often used to compensate for the differences in the timing of the transmission and execution of devices. Buffers are used in terminals, peripheral devices, storage units, and CPUs.

bus the hardware connection that allows data to flow from one component to another (e.g., from the CPU to the line printer).

business intelligence represents those systems that help companies understand what makes the wheels of the corporation turn and to help predict the future impact of current decisions. These systems place a key role in strategic planning process of the corporation. Systems that exemplify business intelligence include medical research, customer profiling, market basket analysis, customer contact analysis, market segmentation, scoring, product profitability, and inventory movement.

business management those systems needed to effectively manage actions resulting from the business intelligence gained. If business intelligence helps companies understand "what" makes the wheels of the corporation turn, business management helps "direct" the wheels as the business landscape changes. To a large extent, these systems augment, extend, and eventually displace capabilities provided by business operations. Systems that exemplify business management include product management, campaign management, inventory management, resource management, and customer information management.

business operations represents those systems that run the day-to-day business. These systems have traditionally make up the legacy environment and provided a competitive advantage by automating manual business processes to gain economies of scale and speed to market. Systems that exemplify business operations include accounts payable, accounts receivable, billing, order processing, compensation, and lead list generation.

byte a basic unit of storage—made up of 8 bits.

C a programming language.

cache a buffer usually built and maintained at the device level. Retrieving data out of a cache is much quicker than retrieving data out of a cylinder.

call to invoke the execution of a module.

canonical model a data model that represents the inherent structure of data without regard to its individual use or hardware or software implementation.

cardinality (of a relation) the number of tuples (i.e., rows) in a relation. *See also* **degree (of a relation).**

CASE Computer Aided Software Engineering.

catalog a directory of all files available to the computer.

chain an organization where records or other items of data are strung together.

chain list a list where the items cannot be located in sequence, but where each item contains an identifier (i.e., pointer) for finding the next item.

channel a subsystem for input to and output from the computer. Data from storage units, for example, flows into the computer by way of a channel.

character a member of the standard set of elements used to represent data in the database.

character type the characters that can represent the value of an attribute.

checkpoint an identified snapshot of the database, or a point at which the transactions against the database have been frozen or have been quiesced.

checkpoint/restart a means of restarting a program at some point other than the beginning—for example, when a failure or interruption has occurred. N checkpoints may be used at intervals throughout an application program. At each of these points, sufficient information is stored to permit the program to be restored to the moment when checkpoint was established.

child a unit of data existing in a 1:n relationship with another unit of data called a parent; where the parent must exist before the child can exist, but the parent can exist even when no child unit of data exists.

CICS (Customer Information Control System) an IBM teleprocessing monitor.

CIO (chief information officer) the manager of all the information processing functions in an organization.

circular file (queue) an organization of data where a finite number of units of data are allocated. Data is then loaded into those units. Upon reaching the end of the allocated units, new data is written over older data at the beginning of the queue. Sometimes called a *wrap-around* queue.

claimed block a second or subsequent physical block of data designated to store table data, after the originally allocated block has run out of space.

class (of entities) all possible entities held by a given proposition.

"CLDS" the facetious name of the system development life cycle of analytical, DSS systems. CLDS is so named because it is the reverse of the name of the classical systems development life cycle—SDLC.

cluster (1) in Teradata, a group of physical devices controlled by the same

AMP; (2) in DB2 and Oracle, the practice of physically colocating data in the same block based on its content.

cluster key the key around which data is clustered in a block (DB2/Oracle).

coalesce to combine two or more sets of items into a single set.

COBOL (COmmon Business Oriented Language) computer language for the business world. A very common language.

CODASYL model a network database model that was originally defined by the Database Task Group (DBTG) of the COnference on DAta SYstem Language (CODASYL) organization.

code (1) to represent data or a computer program in a form that can be accepted by a data processor; (2) to transform data so that it cannot be understood by anyone who does not have the algorithm necessary to decode the data prior to presentation (sometimes called *encode*).

collision the event that occurs when two or more records of data are assigned to the same physical location. Collisions are associated with randomizers or hashers.

column a vertical table where values are selected from the same domain. A row is made up of one or more columns.

command (1) the specification of an activity by the programmer; (2) the actual execution of the specification.

commit a condition raised by the programmer signalling to the DBMS that all update activity done by the program should be executed against a database. Prior to the commit, all update activity can be rolled back or cancelled with no adverse effects on the contents of the database.

commit protocol an algorithm to ensure that a transaction is successfully completed.

commonality of data similar or identical data that occurs in different applications or systems. The recognition and management of commonality of data is one of the foundations of conceptual and physical database design.

communication network the collection of transmission facilities, network processors, and so on, which provides for data movement among terminals and information processors.

compaction a technique for reducing the number of bits required to represent data without losing the contents of the data. With compaction, repetitive data is represented very concisely.

component a data item or array of data items whose component type defines a collection of occurrences with the same data type.

compound index an index spanning multiple columns.

concatenate to link or connect two strings of characters, generally for the purpose of using them as a single value.

conceptual schema a consistent collection of data structures expressing the data needs of the organization. This schema is a comprehensive, base level, and logical description of the environment where an organization exists; free of physical structure and application system considerations.

concurrent operations activities executed simultaneously or during the same time interval.

condensation the process of reducing the volume of data managed without reducing the logical consistency of the data. Condensation is essentially different than compaction.

connect to forge a relationship between two entities, particularly in a network system.

connector a symbol used to indicate that one occurrence of data has a relationship to another occurrence of data. Connectors are used in conceptual database design and can be implemented hierarchically, relationally, in an inverted fashion, or by a network.

content addressable memory main storage that can be addressed by the contents of the data in the memory, as opposed to conventional location addressable memory.

contention the condition that occurs when two or more programs try to access the same data simultaneously.

continuous time span data data organized so that a continuous definition of data over a period of time is represented by one or more records.

control character a character whose occurrence in a particular context initiates, modifies, or stops an operation.

control database a utilitarian database containing data not directly related to the application being built. Typical control databases are audit databases, terminal databases, security databases, etc.

cooperative processing the ability to distribute resources (programs, files, and databases) across the network.

coordinator the two-phase commit protocol defines one database management system as coordinator for the commit process. The coordinator is responsible for communicating with the other database manager involved in a unit of work.

corporate information factory (CIF) is the physical embodiment of the information ecosystem. The CIF was first introduced by W. H. Inmon in the early '80s.

CPU central processing unit.

CPU-bound the state of processing where the computer cannot produce more output, because the CPU portion of the processor is being used at 100 percent capacity. When the computer is CPU-bound, typically the memory and storage processing units are less than 100 percent utilized. With modern DBMS, it is much more likely that the computer is I/O-bound, rather than CPU-bound.

CSP (Cross System Product) an IBM application generator.

CUA (Common User Access) specifies the ways in which the user interface to systems will be constructed.

current value data data whose accuracy is valid as of the moment of execution, as opposed to time-variant data.

cursor (1) an indicator that designates a current position on a screen; (2) a system facility that allows the programmer to thumb from one record to the next after the system has retrieved a set of records.

cursor stability an option that enables data to move under the cursor. Once the program has used the data examined by the cursor, it is released. As opposed to repeatable read.

cylinder the storage area of DASD that can be read without movement of the arm. The term originated with disk files, in which a cylinder consisted of one track on each disk surface so that each of these tracks could have a read/write head positioned over it simultaneously.

DASD *see* **direct access storage device.**

data a recording of facts, concepts, or instructions on a storage medium for communication, retrieval, and processing by automatic means and presentation as information that is understandable by human beings.

data administrator (DA) the individual or organization responsible for the specification, acquisition, and maintenance of data management software and the design, validation, and security of files or databases. The data model and the data dictionary are usually the responsibility of the DA.

data aggregate a collection of data items.

database a collection of interrelated data stored (often with controlled, limited redundancy) according to a schema. A database can serve single or multiple applications.

database administrator (DBA) the organizational function charged with the day-to-day monitoring and care of the databases. The DBA is more closely associated with physical database design than the DA is.

database key a unique value that exists for each record in a database. The value is often indexed, although it can be randomized or hashed.

database machine a dedicated-purpose computer that provides data access and management through total control of the access method, physical storage, and data organization. Often called a *backend processor*. Data is usually managed in parallel by a database machine.

database management system (DBMS) a computer-based software system used to establish and manage data.

database record a physical root and all of its dependents (in IMS).

DatacomDB a database management system created by CA.

data definition the specification of the data entities, their attributes, and their relationships in a coherent database structure to create a schema.

data definition language (DDL) the language used to define the database schema and additional data features that allows the DBMS to generate and manage the internal tables, indexes, buffers, and storage necessary for database processing. Also called a *data description language*.

data description language *see* **data definition language.**

data dictionary a software tool for recording the definition of data, the relationship of one category of data to another, the attributes and keys of groups of data, and so forth.

data division (COBOL) the section of a COBOL program that consists of entries used to define the nature and characteristics of the data to be processed by the program.

data-driven development the approach to development that centers around identifying the commonality of data through a data model and building programs that have a broader scope than the immediate application. Data-driven development differs from traditional application-oriented development which is generally process-driven.

data-driven process a process whose resource consumption depends on the data by which it operates. For example, a hierarchical root has a dependent. For one occurrence, there are two dependents for the root. For another occurrence of the root, there may be 1000 occurrences of the dependent. The same program that accesses the root and all its dependents will use very different amounts of resources when operating against the two roots, although the code will be exactly the same.

data element (1) an attribute of an entity; (2) a uniquely named and well-defined category of data that consists of data items, and that is included in the record of an activity.

data engineering the planning and building of data structures according to accepted mathematical models on the basis of the inherent characteristics of the data itself, and independent of hardware and software systems. *See also* **information engineering.**

data independence the property of being able to modify the overall logical and physical structure of data without changing any of the application code supporting the data.

data item a discrete representation having the properties that define the data element to which it belongs. *See also* **data element.**

data item set (dis) a grouping of data items, each of which directly relates to the key of the grouping of data in which the data items reside. The data item set is found in the mid-level model.

data manipulation language (DML) (1) a programming language that is supported by a DBMS and used to access a database; (2) language constructs added to a higher-order language (e.g., COBOL) for the purpose of database manipulation.

data mart contains data from the Data Warehouse tailored to support the specific analytical requirements of a given business unit. This business unit could be defined to be as broad as a division or as narrow as a department.

data model (1) the logical data structures, including operations and constraints provided by a DBMS for effective database processing; (2) the system used for the representation of data (e.g., the ERD or relational model).

data record an identifiable set of data values treated as a unit, an occurrence of a schema in a database, or a collection of atomic data items describing a specific object, event, or tuple.

data security the protection of the data in a database against unauthorized disclosure, alteration, or destruction. There are different levels of security.

data set a named collection of logically related data items, arranged in a prescribed manner, and described by control information; to which the programming systems has access.

data storage description language (DSDL) a language to define the organization of stored data in terms of an operating system and device-independent storage environment. *See also* **device media control language.**

data structure a logical relationship among data elements that is designed to support specific data manipulation functions (e.g., trees, lists, and tables).

data type the definition of a set of representable values that is primitive and without meaningful logical subdivision.

data view *see* **user view.**

data volatility the rate of change of the contents of data.

data warehouse a collection of integrated subject-oriented databases designed to support the DSS function, where each unit of data is relevant to some moment in time. The data warehouse contains atomic data and lightly summarized data.

data warehouse administrator (DWA) represents the organization responsible for managing the data warehouse environment.

DB2 a database management system created by IBM.

DB/DC database/data communications.

DBMS language interface (DB I/O module) software that applications invoke in order to access a database. The module in turn has direct access with the DBMS. Standard enforcement and standard error checking are often features of an I/O module.

deadlock *see* **deadly embrace.**

deadly embrace the event that occurs when transaction A desires to access data currently protected by transaction B, while at the same time transaction B desires to access data that is currently being protected by transaction A. The deadly embrace condition is a serious impediment to performance.

decision support system (DSS) a system used to support managerial decisions. Usually DSS involves the analysis of many units of data in a heuristic fashion. As a rule, DSS processing does not involve the update of data.

decompaction the opposite of compaction; once data is stored in a compacted form, it must be decompacted to be used.

decryption the opposite of encryption. Once data is stored in an encrypted fashion, it must be decrypted to be used.

degree (of a relation) the number of attributes or columns of a relation. *See also* **cardinality of a relation.**

delimiter a flag, symbol, or convention used to mark the boundaries of a record, field, or other unit of storage.

demand staging the movement of blocks of data from one storage device to another device with a shorter access time, when programs request the blocks and the blocks are not already in the faster access storage.

denormalization the technique of placing normalized data in a physical location that optimizes the performance of the system.

derived data data whose existence depends on two or more occurrences of a major subject of the enterprise.

derived data element a data element that is not necessarily stored, but that can be generated when needed (e.g., age as of current date and date of birth).

derived relation a relation that can be obtained from previously defined relations by applying some sequence of retrieval and derivation operations (e.g., a table that is the combination of others and some projections). *See also* **a virtual relation.**

design review the quality assurance process where all aspects of a system are reviewed publicly prior to the striking of code.

device media control language (DMCL) a language used to define the mapping of the data onto the physical storage media. *See also* **data storage description language.**

direct access retrieval or storage of data by reference to its location on a volume. The access mechanism goes directly to the data in question, as is generally required with online use of data. Also called *random access* or *hashed access.*

direct access storage device (DASD) a data storage unit where data can be accessed directly without having to progress through a serial file such as a magnetic tape file. A disk unit is a direct access storage device.

directory a table specifying the relationships between items of data. Sometimes it is a table or index giving the addresses of data.

distributed catalog a distributed catalog is needed to achieve site autonomy. The catalog at each site maintains information about objects in the local databases. The distributed catalog keeps information on replicated and distributed tables stored at that site and on remote tables located at another site that cannot be accessed locally.

distributed database a database controlled by a central DBMS, but where the storage devices are geographically dispersed or not attached to the same processor. *See also* **parallel I/O.**

distributed environment a set of related data processing systems, where each system has capacity to operate autonomously, but where applications can execute at multiple sites. Some of the systems may be connected with teleprocessing links into a network in which each system is a node.

distributed free space space left empty at intervals in a data layout, to permit insertion of new data.

distributed request a transaction across multiple nodes.

distributed unit of work the work done by a transaction that operates against multiple nodes.

division an operation that partitions a relation on the basis of the contents of data found in the relation.

DL/1 IBM's Data Language One, used for describing logical and physical data structures.

domain the set of legal values from which actual values are derived for an attribute or a data element.

download the stripping of data from one database to another, based on the content of data found in the first database.

drill-down analysis the type of analysis where examination of a summary number leads to the exploration of the components of the sum.

dual database the practice of separating high-performance, transaction-oriented data from decision support data.

dual database management systems the practice of using multiple database management systems to control different aspects of the database environment.

dumb terminal a device used to interact directly with the end user, where all processing is done on a remote computer. A dumb terminal acts as a device that gathers data and displays data only.

dynamic SQL SQL statements that are prepared and executed within a program, while the program is executing. In dynamic SQL, the SQL source is contained in host language variables rather than being coded into the application program.

dynamic storage allocation a technique where the storage areas assigned to computer programs are determined during processing.

dynamic subset of data a subset of data selected by a program and operated on only by the program, and released by the program once it ceases execution.

EDI Electronic Data Interchange.

EIS (Executive Information Systems) systems designed for the top executives, featuring drill-down analysis and trend analysis.

embedded pointer a record pointer (i.e., a means of internally linking related records) that is not available to an external index or directory. Embedded pointers are used to reduce search time, but also require maintenance overhead.

encoding a shortening or abbreviation of the physical representation of a data value (e.g., male = "M", female = "F").

encryption the transformation of data from a recognizable form to a form unrecognizable without the algorithm used for the encryption. Encryption is usually done for the purpose of security.

enterprise the generic term for the company, corporation, agency, or business unit. Usually associated with data modelling.

entity a person, place, or thing of interest to the data modeller at the highest level of abstraction.

entity-relationship attribute (ERA) model a data model that defines entities, the relationship between the entities, and the attributes that have values to describe the properties of entities and/or relationships.

entity-relationship diagram (ERD) a high-level data model—the schematic showing all the entities within the scope of integration and the direct relationship between those entities.

event a signal that an activity of significance has occurred. An event is noted by the information system.

event discrete data data relating to the measurement or description of an event.

expert system a system that captures and automates the usage of human experience and intelligence.

extent (1) a list of unsigned integers that specifies an array; (2) a physical unit of disk storage attached to a data set after the initial allocation of data has been made.

external data (1) data originating from other than the operational systems of a corporation; (2) data residing outside the central processing complex.

external schema a logical description of a user's method of organizing and structuring data. Some attributes or relationships can be omitted from the corresponding conceptual schema or can be renamed or otherwise transformed. *See also* **view.**

extract the process of selecting data from one environment and transporting it to another environment.

field *see* **data item.**

file a set of related records treated as a unit and stored under a single logical file name.

first in first out (FIFO) a fundamental ordering of processing in a queue.

first in last out (FILO) a standard order of processing in a stack.

flag an indicator or character that signals the occurrence of some condition.

flat file a collection of records containing no data aggregates, nested repeated data items, or groups of data items.

floppy disk a device for storing data on a personal computer.

foreign key an attribute that is not a primary key in a relational system, but whose values are the values of the primary key of another relation.

format the arrangement or layout of data in or on a data medium or in a program definition.

forward recovery a recovery technique that restores a database by reapplying all transactions using a before image from a specified point in time to a copy of the database taken at that moment in time.

fourth-generation language language or technology designed to allow the end user unfettered access to data.

functional decomposition the division of operations into hierarchical functions (i.e., activities) that form the basis for procedures.

granularity the level of detail contained in a unit of data. The more detail there is, the lower the level of granularity. The less detail there is, the higher the level of granularity.

graphic a symbol produced on a screen representing an object or a process in the real world.

hash to convert the value of the key of a record into a location on disk.

hash total a total of the values of one or more fields, used for the purposes of auditability and control.

header record or header table a record containing common, constant, or identifying information for a group of records that follow.

heuristic the mode of analysis in which the next step is determined by the results of the current step of analysis. Used for decision support processing.

hierarchical model a data model providing a tree structure for relating data elements or groups of data elements. Each node in the structure represents a group of data elements or a record type. There can be only one root node at the start of the hierarchical structure.

hit an occurrence of data that satisfies some search criteria.

hit ratio a measure of the number of records in a file expected to be accessed in a given run. Usually expressed as a percentage—number of input transactions/number of records in the file $\times$ 100 = hit ratio.

homonyms identical names that refer to different attributes.

horizontal distribution the splitting of a table across different sites by rows. With horizontal distribution rows of a single table reside at different sites in a distributed database network.

host the processor receiving and processing a transaction.

Huffman code a code for data compaction in which frequently used characters are encoded with fewer bits than infrequently used characters.

IDMS a network DBMS from CA.

IEEE Institute of Electrical and Electronics Engineers.

image copy a procedure in which a database is physically copied to another medium for the purposes of backup.

IMS Information Management System—an operational DBMS by IBM.

index the portion of the storage structure maintained to provide efficient access to a record when its index key item is known.

index chains chains of data within an index.

indexed sequential access method (ISAM) a file structure and access method in which records can be processed sequentially (e.g., in order, by key) or by directly looking up their locations on a table, thus making it unnecessary to process previously inserted records.

index point a hardware reference mark on a disk or drum; used for timing purposes.

indirect addressing any method of specifying or locating a record through calculation (e.g., locating a record through the scan of an index).

information data that human beings assimilate and evaluate to solve problems or make decisions.

information center the organizational unit charged with identifying and accessing information needed in DSS processing.

information ecosystem a comprehensive information solution that complements traditional Business Intelligence (i.e., analytics) with capabilities to deliver Business Management (i.e., customer care, account consolidation, etc.). This will allow companies to capitalize on a changing business landscape characterized by customer relationships and customized product delivery.

information engineering (IE) the discipline of creating a data-driven development environment.

input/output (I/O) the means by which data is stored and/or retrieved on DASD. I/O is measured in milliseconds (i.e., mechanical speeds) whereas computer processing is measured in nanoseconds (i.e., electronic speeds).

instances a set of values representing a specific entity belonging to a particular entity type. A single value is also the instance of a data item.

integrity the property of a database that ensures that the data contained in the database is as accurate and consistent as possible.

intelligent database a database that contains shared logic as well as shared data and automatically invokes that logic when the data is accessed. Logic, constraints, and controls relating to the use of the data are represented in an intelligent data model.

interactive a mode of processing that combines some of the characteristics of online transaction processing and batch processing. In interactive processing, the end user interacts with data over which he or she has exclusive control. In addition, the end user can initiate background activity to be run against the data.

interleaved data data from different tables mixed into a simple table space, where there is commonality of physical colocation based on a common key value.

internal schema the schema that describes logical structures of the data and the physical media over which physical storage is mapped.

interpretive a mode of data manipulation in which the commands to the DBMS are translated as the user enters them (as opposed to the programmed mode of process manipulation).

intersection data data that is associated with the junction of two or more record types or entities, but which has no meaning when disassociated with any records or entities forming the junction.

inverted file a file structure that uses an inverted index, where entries are grouped according to the content of the key being referenced. Inverted files provide for the fast spontaneous searching of files.

inverted index an index structure organized by means of a nonunique key, to speed the search for data by content.

inverted list a list organized around a secondary index instead of around a primary key.

I/O (Input/Output Operation) Input/output operations are the key to performance because they operate at mechanical speeds, not at electronic speeds.

I/O bound the point after which no more processing can be done because the I/O subsystem is saturated.

ISAM *see* **indexed sequential access method.**

"is a type of" an analytical tool used in abstracting data during the process of conceptual database design (e.g., a cocker spaniel is a type of dog).

ISDN (Integrated Services Digital Network) telecommunications technology that enables companies to transfer data and voice through the same phone lines.

ISO International Standards Organization.

item *see* **data item.**

item type a classification of an item according to its domain, generally in a gross sense.

iterative analysis the mode of processing in which the next step of processing depends on the results obtained by the existing step in execution; heuristic processing.

JAD (Joint Application Design) an organization of people—usually end users—to create and refine application system requirements.

join an operation that takes two relations as operands and produces a new relation by concatenating the tuples and matching the corresponding columns when a stated condition holds between the two.

judgement sample a sample of data where it is accepted or rejected for the sample based on one or more parameters.

junction from the network environment, an occurrence of data that has two or more parent segments. For example, an order for supplies must have a supplier parent and a part parent.

justify to adjust the value representation in a character field to the right or to the left, ignoring blanks encountered.

keeplist a sequence of database keys maintained by the DBMS for the duration of the session.

key a data item or combination of data items used to identify or locate a record instance (or other similar data groupings).

key compression a technique for reducing the number of bits in keys; used in making indexes occupy less space.

key, primary a unique attribute used to identify a single record in a database.

key, secondary a nonunique attribute used to identify a class of records in a database.

label a set of symbols used to identify or describe an item, record, message, or file. Occasionally, a label may be the same as the address of the record in storage.

language a set of characters, conventions, and rules used to convey information, and consisting of syntax and semantics.

latency the time taken by a DASD device to position the read arm over the physical storage medium. For general purposes, average latency time is used.

least frequently used (LFU) a replacement strategy in which new data must replace existing data in an area of storage; the least frequently used items are replaced.

least recently used (LRU) a replacement strategy in which new data must replace existing data in an area of storage; the least recently used items are replaced.

level of abstraction the level of abstraction appropriate to a dimension. The level of abstraction that is appropriate is entirely dependent on the ultimate user of the system.

line the hardware by which data flows to or from the processor. Lines typically go to terminals, printers, and other processors.

line polling the activity of the teleprocessing monitor in which different lines are queried to determine whether they have data and/or transactions that need to be transmitted.

line time the length of time required for a transaction to go either from the terminal to the processor or the processor to the terminal. Typically line time is the single largest component of online response time.

linkage the ability to relate one unit of data to another.

linked list set of records in which each record contains a pointer to the next record on the list. *See also* **chain.**

list an ordered set of data items.

living sample a representative database typically used for heuristic statistical analytical processing in place of a large database. Periodically the very large database is selectively stripped of data so that the resulting living sample database represents a cross section of the very large database at some moment in time.

load to insert data values into a database that was previously empty.

local site support within a distributed unit of work, a local site update allows a process to perform SQL update statements referring to the local site.

local transaction in a distributed DBMS, a transaction that requires reference only to data that is stored at the site where the transaction originated.

locality of processing in distributed database, the design of processing so that remote access of data is eliminated or reduced substantively.

lockup the event that occurs when update is done against a database record, and the transaction has not yet reached a commit point. The online transaction needs to prevent other transactions from accessing the data while update is occurring.

log a journal of activity.

logging the automatic recording of data with regard to the access of the data, the updates to the data, etc.

logical representation a data view or description that does not depend on a physical storage device or a computer program.

loss of identity when data is brought in from an external source and the identity of the external source is discarded, loss of identity occurs. A common practice with microprocessor data.

LU6.2 (Logical Unit Type 6.2) peer-to-peer data stream with network operating system for program-to-program communication. LU6.2 allows midrange machines to talk to one another without the involvement of the mainframe.

machine learning the ability of a machine to improve its performance automatically, based on past performance.

magnetic tape (1) the storage medium most closely associated with sequential processing; (2) a large ribbon on which magnetic images are stored and retrieved.

main storage database (MSDB) a database that resides entirely in main storage. Such databases are very fast to access, but require special handling at the time of update. Another limitation of MSDBs are that they can only manage small amounts of data.

master file a file that holds the system of record for a given set of data (usually bound by an application).

maximum transaction arrival rate (MTAR) the rate of arrival of transactions at the moment of peak period processing.

message (1) the data input by the user in the online environment that is used to drive a transaction; (2) the output of a transaction.

metadata (1) data about data; (2) the description of the structure, content, keys, indexes, etc. of data.

metalanguage a language used to specify other languages.

metaprocess descriptive information about the code or process(es) that act against data.

microprocessor a small processor serving the needs of a single user.

migration the process by which frequently used items of data are moved to more readily accessible areas of storage and infrequently used items of data are moved to less readily accessible areas of storage.

mips (million instructions per second) the standard measurement of processor speed for minicomputers and mainframe computers.

mode of operation a classification for systems that execute in a similar fashion and share distinctive operational characteristics. Some modes of operation are: operational, DSS, online, interactive, etc.

modulo an arithmetic term describing the remainder of a division process. 10 modulo 7 is 3. Modulo is usually associated with the randomization process.

MOLAP multidimensional online analytical processing supports OLAP using specialized, proprietary multidimensional database technology.

multilist organization a chained file organization in which the chains are divided into fragments and each fragment is indexed. This organization of data permits faster access to the data.

multiple key retrieval that requires searches of data on the basis of the values of several key fields (some or all of which are secondary keys).

MVS (Multiple Virtual Storage) IBM's mainline operating system for mainframe processors. There are several extensions of MVS.

Named Pipes program-to-program protocol with Microsoft's LAN Manager. The Named Pipes API supports intra- and inter-machine process-to-process communications.

natural forms first normal form—data that has been organized into two-dimensional flat files without repeating groups. Second normal form—data that functionally depends on the entire candidate key. Third normal form—data that has had all transitive dependencies on data items other than the candidate key removed. Fourth normal form—data whose candidate key is related to all data items in the record, and that contains no more than one nontrivial multivalued dependency on the candidate key.

natural join a join in which the redundant logic components generated by the join are removed.

natural language a language generally spoken, whose rules are based on current usage and not explicitly defined by grammar.

navigate to steer a course through a database, from record to record, by means of an algorithm which examines the content of data.

network a computer network consists of a collection of circuits, data-switching elements, and computing systems. The switching devices in the network are called communication processors. A network provides a configuration for computer systems and communication facilities within which data can be stored and accessed, and within which DBMS can operate.

network model a data model that provides data relationships on the basis of records and groups of records (i.e., sets) in which one record is designated as the set owner and a single member record can belong to one or more sets.

nine's complement transformation of a numeric field calculated by subtracting the initial value from a field consisting of all nines.

node a point in the network at which data is switched.

nonprocedural language syntax that directs the computer as to what to do, not how to do it. Typical nonprocedural languages include RAMIS, FOCUS, NOMAD, and SQL.

normalize to decompose complex data structures into natural structures.

null an item or record for which no value currently exists or possibly may ever exist.

numeric a representation using only numbers and the decimal point.

occurrence *see* **instances.**

offset pointer an indirect pointer. An offset pointer exists inside a block and the index points to the offset. If data must be moved, only the offset pointer in the block must be altered; the index entry remains untouched.

OLAP online analytical processing is a category of software technology that enables analysts, managers and executives to perform ad hoc data access and analysis based on its dimensionality. This form of multidimensional analysis provides business insight through fast, consistent, interactive access to a wide variety of possible views of information.

online storage storage devices and storage mediums where data can be accessed in a direct fashion.

operating system software that enables a computer to supervise its own operations and automatically call in programs, routines, languages, and data as needed for continuous operation throughout the execution of different types of jobs.

operational data data used to support the daily processing a company does.

operations the department charged with the running of the computer.

optical disk a storage medium using lasers as opposed to magnetic devices. Optical disk is typically write-only, is much less expensive per byte than magnetic storage, and is highly reliable.

ORACLE a DBMS by ORACLE Corp.

order to place items in an arrangement specified by rules such as numeric or alphabetic order. *see* **sort.**

OS/2 the operating system for IBM's Personal System.

OSF Open Software Foundation.

OSI Open Systems Interconnection overflow (1) the condition in which a record or a segment cannot be stored in its home address because the address is already occupied. In this case, the data is placed in another location referred to as overflow; (2) the area of DASD where data is sent when the overflow condition is triggered.

ownership the responsibility for updating for operational data.

padding a technique used to fill a field, record, or block with default data (e.g., blanks or zeros).

page (1) a basic unit of data on DASD; (2) a basic unit of storage in main memory.

page fault a program interruption that occurs when a page that is referred to is not in main memory and must be read in from external storage.

page fixed the state in which programs or data cannot be removed from main storage. Only a limited amount of storage can be page fixed.

paging in virtual storage systems, the technique of making memory appear to be larger than it really is by transferring blocks (pages) of data or programs into external memory.

parallel data organization an arrangement of data in which the data is spread over independent storage devices and is managed independently.

parallel I/O the process of accessing or storing data on multiple physical data devices.

parallel search storage a storage device in which one or more parts of all storage locations are queried simultaneously for a certain condition or under certain parameters. *See also* **associative storage.**

parameter an elementary data value used as a criteria for qualification, usually of searches of data or in the control of modules.

parent a unit of data in a 1:n relationship with another unit of data called a child, where the parent can exist independently, but the child cannot exist unless there is a parent.

parsing the algorithm that translates syntax into meaningful machine instructions. Parsing determines the meaning of statements issued in the data manipulation language.

partition a segmentation technique in which data is divided into physically different units. Partitioning can be done at the application or the system level.

path length the number of instructions executed for a given program or instruction.

peak period the time when the most transactions arrive at the computer with the expectation of execution.

performance the length of time from the moment a request is issued until the first of the results of the request are received.

periodic discrete data a measurement or description of data taken at a regular time interval.

physical representation (1) the representation and storage of data on a medium such as magnetic storage; (2) the description of data that depends on such physical factors as length of elements, records, pointers, etc.

pipes vehicles for passing data from one application to another.

plex or network structure a relationship between records or other groupings of data in which a child record can have more than one parent record.

plug compatible manufacturer (PCM) a manufacturer of equipment that functionally is identical to that of another manufacturer (usually IBM).

pointer the address of a record, or other groupings of data contained in another record, so that a program may access the former record when it has retrieved the latter record. The address can be absolute, relative, or symbolic, and hence the pointer is referred to as absolute, relative, or symbolic.

pools the buffers made available to the online controller.

populate to place occurrences of data values in a previously empty database. *See also* **load.**

precision the degree of discrimination with which a quantity is stated. For example, a three-digit numeral discriminates among 1000 possibilities, from 000 to 999.

precompilation the processing of source text prior to compilation. In an SQL environment, SQL statements are replaced with statements that will be recognized by the host language compiler.

prefix data data in a segment or a record used exclusively for system control; usually unavailable to the user.

primary key *see* **key, primary.**

primitive data data whose existence depends on only a single occurrence of a major subject area of the enterprise.

privacy the prevention of unauthorized access and manipulation of data.

privilege descriptor a persistent object used by a DBMS to enforce constraints on operations.

problems database the component of a DSS application where previously defined decision parameters are stored. A problems database is consulted to review characteristics of past decisions and to determine ways to meet current decision-making needs.

processor the hardware at the center of execution of computer programs. Generally speaking, processors are divided into three categories—mainframes, minicomputers, and microcomputers.

processor cycles the hardware's internal cycles that drive the computer (e.g., initiate I/O, perform logic, move data, perform arithmetic functions, etc.).

production environment the environment where operational, high-performance processing is run.

program a set of instructions that tell the computer what to do. Programs are sometimes referred to as applications and/or software.

program area the portion of main memory in which application programs are executed.

progressive overflow a method of handling overflow in a randomly organized file that does not require the use of pointers. An overflow record is stored in the first available space and is retrieved by a forward serial search from the home address.

projection an operation that takes one relation as an operand and returns a second relation that consists of only the selected attributes or columns, with duplicate rows eliminated.

proposition a statement about entities that asserts or denies that some condition holds for those entities.

protocol the call format used by a teleprocessing monitor.

punched cards an early storage medium on which data and input were stored. Today punched cards are rare.

purge data the data on or after which a storage area may be overwritten. Used in conjunction with a file label, it is a means of protecting file data until an agreed-upon release date is reached.

query language a language that enables an end user to interact directly with a DBMS to retrieve and possibly modify data managed under the DBMS.

record an aggregation of values of data organized by their relation to a common key.

record-at-a-time processing the access of data a record at a time, a tuple at a time, etc.

recovery the restoration of the database to an original position or condition, often after major damage to the physical medium.

redundancy the practice of storing more than one occurrence of data. In the case where data can be updated, redundancy poses serious problems. In the case where data is not updated, redundancy is often a valuable and necessary design tool.

referential integrity the facility of a DBMS to ensure the validity of a predefined relationship.

reorganization the process of unloading data in a poorly organized state and reloading the data in a well-organized state. Reorganization in some DBMS is used to restructure data. Reorganization is often called *reorg* or an *unload/reload* process.

repeating groups a collection of data that can occur several times within a given record occurrence.

ROLAP relational online analytical processing supports OLAP using techniques that allow multidimensionality to be implemented in a two dimensional RDBMS. Star join schema is a common database design technique used in this environment.

rolling summary a form of storing archival data where the most recent data has the lowest level of detail stored and the older data has higher levels of detail stored.

scope of integration the formal definition of the boundaries of the system being modelled.

SDLC (System Development Life Cycle) the classical operational system development life cycle that typically includes requirements gathering, analysis, design, programming, testing, integration, and implementation. Sometimes called a *waterfall* development life cycle.

sequential file a file in which records are ordered according to the values of one or more key fields. The records can be processed in this sequence starting from the first record in the file, and continuing to the last record in the file.

serial file a sequential file in which the records are physically adjacent, in sequential order.

set-at-a-time processing access of data by groups, each member of which satisfies some selection criteria.

snapshot a database dump or the archiving of data as of some one moment in time.

star join schema a relational database design technique that organizes data around its multidimensionality in terms of business dimensions and measurements (a.k.a., facts).

storage hierarchy storage units linked to form a storage subsystem, in which some units are fast to access and consume small amounts of storage, but which are expensive, and other units are slow to access and are large, but are inexpensive to store.

subject database a database organized around a major subject of the corporation. Classical subject databases are for customer, transaction, product, part, vendor, etc.

system log an audit trail of relevant system events (for example, transaction entries, database changes, etc.).

system of record the definitive and singular source of operational data. If data element abc has a value of 25 in a database record, but a value of 45 in the system of record, by definition the first value must be incorrect. The system of record is useful for the management of redundancy of data.

table a relation that consists of a set of columns with a heading and a set of rows (i.e., tuples).

time stamping the practice of tagging each record with some moment in time, usually when the record was created or when the record was passed from one environment to another.

time-variant data data whose accuracy is relevant to some moment in time. The three common forms of time-variant data are continuous time span data, event discrete data, and periodic discrete data. *See also* **current value data.**

transition data data possessing both primitive and derived characteristics; usually very sensitive to the running of the business. Typical transition data include interest rates for a bank, policy rates for an insurance company, retail sale prices for a manufacturer/distributor, etc.

trend analysis the process of looking at homogeneous data over a spectrum of time.

true archival data data at the lowest level of granularity in the current level detail database.

update to change, add, delete, or replace values in all or selected entries, groups, or attributes stored in a database.

user a person or process issuing commands or messages and receiving stimuli from the information system.

Recommended Reading

ARTICLES

Adelman, Sid. "The Data Warehouse Database Explosion." *DMR* (December 1996). A very good discussion of why volumes of data are growing as fast as they are in the data warehouse environment and what can be done about it.

"An Architecture for a Business and Information System." *IBM Systems Journal* 17, no. 1 (1988). A description of IBM's understanding of the data warehouse.

Ashbrook, Jim. "Information Preservation." *CIO Magazine* (July 1993). An executive's view of the data warehouse.

Bair, John. "It's about Time! Supporting Temporal Data in a Warehouse." *INFODB* 10, no. 1 (February 1996). A good discussion of some of the aspects of time-variant data in the DSS/data warehouse environment.

Ballinger, Carrie. "TPC's Emerging Benchmark for Decision Support." *DBMS* (December 1993). A description of the extension of the TPC benchmark to include DSS.

Discount Store News. "Retail Technology Charges Up at KMart." (February 17, 1992). A description of the technology employed by KMart for its data warehouse, ODS environment.

Geiger, Jon. "Data Element Definition." *DMR* (December 1996). A good description of the definitions required in the system of record.

Geiger, Jon. "Information Management for Competitive Advantage." *Strategic Systems Journal* (June 1993). A discussion of how the data warehouse and the Zachman framework have advanced the state-of-the art.

Geiger, Jon. "What's in a Name." *Data Management Review* (June 1996). A discussion of the implications of naming structures in the data warehouse environment.

Gilbreah, Roy, Jill Schilp, and Robert Rickton. "Towards an Outcomes Management Informational Processing Architecture." *HealthCare Information Management* 10., no. 1 (spring 1996). A discussion of the architected environment as it relates to health care.

Gilbreath, Roy. "Health Care Data Repositories: Components and a Model." *Journal of the Healthcare Information and Management Systems Society* 9, no. 1 (Spring 1995). An excellent description of information architecture as it relates to health care.

Gilbreath, Roy. "Informational Processing Architecture for Outcomes Management." A description of the data warehouse as it applies to health care and outcomes analysis. Under review.

Goldberg, Paula, Robert Lambert, and Katherine Powell. "Guidelines for Defining Requirements for Decision Support Systems." *Data Resource Management Journal* (October 1991). A good description of how to define end-user requirements before building the data warehouse.

Graham, Stephen, analyst. "The Foundations of Wisdom." IDC Special Report (April 1996). International Data Corp. (Toronto, Canada). The definitive study on the return on investment for the data warehouse, as well as the measurement of cost effectiveness.

Graham, Stephen "The Financial Impact of Data Warehousing." *Data Management Review* (June 1996). A description of the cost-benefit analysis report done by IDC.

Hackney, Doug. "Vendors Are Our Friends." *Data Management Review* (June 1996). Doug Hackney talks about beneficial relationships with vendors.

Hufford, Duane. "A Conceptual Model for Documenting Data Synchronization Requirements." American Management Systems Data synchronization and the data warehouse.

Hufford, Duane. "Data Administration Support for Business Process Improvement." American Management Systems. The data warehouse and data administration.

Hufford, Duane. "Data Warehouse Quality, Part I." *Data Management Review* (January 1996). A description of data warehouse quality.

Hufford, Duane. "Data Warehouse Quality—Part II." *Data Management Review* (March 1996). The second part of the discussion on data quality.

Imhoff, Claudia, and Jon Geiger. "Data Quality in the Data Warehouse." *Data Management Review* (April 1996). A description of the parameters used to gauge the quality of data warehouse data.

Imhoff, Claudia. "End Users: Use 'em or Lose 'em." *DMR* (November 1996). An excellent discussion of the ways to manage the end-user data warehouse effort.

Imhoff, Claudia and Ryan Sousa, "Information Ecosystem–Introduction," *Data Management Review* (January 1997) Introduction to the information ecosystem.

Imhoff, Claudia and Ryan Sousa, "Information Ecosystem–Corporate Information Factory," *Data Management Review* (February 1997) Details the parts and pieces of the Corporate Information Factory as defined by Bill Inmon. In addition, reviews the business relevance of the capabilities produced.

Imhoff, Claudia and Ryan Sousa, "Information Ecosystem–Administration," *Data Management Review* (March 1997) Details the components and techniques used in administering the information ecosystem.

Imhoff, Claudia and Ryan Sousa, "Information Ecosystem–People & Process," *Data Management Review* (April 1997) Details suggested organizational structures and roles. Additionally reviews processes for building, using and managing the information ecosystem.

Imhoff, Claudia and Ryan Sousa, "Information Ecosystem–Information Services," *Data Management Review* (May 1997) Discusses how Information Services is used to provide a common navigation interface to the information ecosystem (Metadata, Data Delivery, DSS tools, etc.), how this interface facilitates the coordination of People & Process and how it ultimately provides a common knowledge fabric.

Imhoff, Claudia and Jon Geiger, "Data Quality in the Data Warehouse," *Data Management Review* (April 1996) Provides insights and guidelines for defining and measuring quality in the data warehouse environment.

Imhoff, Claudia. "Data Steward," *ComputerWorld* (September 4, 1995) Provides an overview of the data steward's role in the data warehouse environment. Additionally, this role is contrasted to the traditional role of a data analyst.

"In the Words of Father Inmon." *MIS* (February 1996). An interview with Bill Inmon in November of 1995 in Australia.

Inmon W. H. "Data Structures in the Information Warehouse." *Enterprise Systems Journal* (January 1992). A description of the common data structures found in the data warehouse.

Inmon, W. H. "At the Heart of the Matter." *Data Base Programming/Design* (July 1988). Primitive and derived data and what the differences are.

Inmon, W. H. "Building the Data Bridge." *Data Base Programming/Design* (April 1992). Ten critical success factors in building the data warehouse.

Inmon, W. H. "Chargeback in the Information Warehouse." *Data Management Review* (March 1993). Chargeback in the data warehouse can be both a blessing and a curse. This article addresses both sides of the issue.

Inmon, W. H. "Choosing the Correct Approach to Data Warehousing: 'Big Bang' vs Iterative." *Data Management Review* (March 1996). A discussion of the proper strategic approach to data warehousing.

Inmon, W. H. "Commentary: The Migration Path." *ComputerWorld* (July 29, 1996). A brief description of some of the issues of migrating to the data warehouse.

Inmon, W. H. "Cost Justification in the Data Warehouse." *Data Management Review* (June 1996). A discussion of how to justify DSS and data warehouse on the cost of reporting.

Inmon, W. H. "Data Warehouse and Contextual Data: Pioneering a New Dimension." *Data Base Newsletter* 23, no. 4 (July/August 1995). A description of the need for contextual data over time, as found in the data warehouse.

Inmon, W. H. "Data Warehouse Lays Foundation for Bringing Data Investment Forward." *Application Development Trends* (January 1994). A description of the data warehouse and the relation to legacy systems.

Inmon, W. H. "Data Warehouse Security: Encrypting Data." *Data Management Review* (November 1996). A description of some of the challenges of data warehouse security and industrial strength security.

Inmon, W. H. "Data Warehouse—A Perspective of Data over Time." *370/390 Data Base Management* (February 1992). A description of the relationship of the data warehouse and the management of data over time.

Inmon, W. H. "EIS and Detail." *Data Management Review* (January 1995). A description of how much detail is needed to support EIS and the role of summarized data in the data warehouse environment.

Inmon, W. H. "EIS and the Data Warehouse." *Data Base Programming/Design* (November 1992). The relationship between EIS and the data warehouse.

Inmon, W. H. "From Transactions to the Operational Data Store." *INFO DB* (December 1995). A discussion about how quickly transactions in the operational environment go into the operational data store.

Inmon, W. H. "Going Against the Grain." *Data Base Programming/Design* (July 1990). A description of the granularity issue and how it relates to the data warehouse.

Inmon, W. H. "Growth in the Data Warehouse." *Data Management Review* (December 1995). A description of why the data warehouse grows so fast and the phenomenon of increasing amounts of storage while decreasing the percent utilization of storage.

Inmon, W. H. "Knowing Your DSS End-User: Tourists, Explorers, Farmers." *DMR* (October 1996). A description of the different categories of end users.

Inmon, W. H. "Managing the Data Warehouse Environment." *Data Management Review* (February 1996). Defining who the data warehouse administrator is.

Inmon, W. H. "Managing the Data Warehouse: The Data Content Card Catalog." *DMR* (December 1996). An introduction to the notion of a data content card catalog, i.e., stratification of data content.

Inmon, W. H. "Measuring Capacity in the Data Warehouse." *Enterprise Systems Journal* (August 1996). A discussion of how capacity should be measured in the data warehouse, DSS environment.

Inmon, W. H. "Metadata: A Checkered Past, A Bright Future." *370/390 Data Base Management* (July 1992). A conversation about metadata and how metadata relates to the data warehouse.

Inmon, W. H. "Monitoring the Data Warehouse Environment." *Data Management Review* (January 1996). What is a data monitor for the data warehouse environment and why would you need it?

Inmon, W. H. "Multidimensional Data Bases and Data Warehousing." *Data Management Review* (February 1995). A description of how current detailed data in the data warehouse fits with multidimensional DBMS.

Inmon, W. H. "Neat Little Packages." *Data Base Programming/Design* (August 1992). A description of how data relationships are treated in the data warehouse.

Inmon, W. H. "Now Which Is Data, Which Is Information." *Data base Programming/Design* (May 1993). The difference between data and information.

Inmon, W. H. "Performance in the Data Warehouse Environment." *Data Warehouse Report* Issue 3 (Autumn 1995). A description of the different aspects of performance in the data warehouse environment.

Inmon, W. H. "Performance in the Data Warehouse Environment—Part 2." *Data Warehouse Report* (Winter 1995). A continuation of the prior article on data warehouse performance.

Inmon, W. H. "Profile/Aggregate Records in the Data Warehouse." *Data management Review* (July 1995). A description of how profile/aggregate records are created and used in the data warehouse environment.

Inmon, W. H. "Profiling the DSS Analyst." *Data Management Review* (March 1995). A description of DSS analysts as farmers and explorers.

Inmon, W. H. "Rethinking Data Relationships for Warehouse Design." *Sybase Server* 5, no. 1 (Spring 1996). A discussion of the issues of data warehouse data relationships.

Inmon, W. H. "SAP and the Data Warehouse." *DMR* (July/Aug 1996). A description of why data warehouse is still needed in the face of SAP.

Inmon, W. H. "Security in the Data Warehouse: Data Privatization." *Enterprise Systems Journal* (March 1996). Data warehouse requires a very different approach to security than the traditional VIEW based approach offered by DBMS vendors.

Inmon, W. H. "Summary Data: The New Frontier." *Data Management Review* (May 1996). A description of the different types of summary data including dynamic summary data and static summary data, lightly summarized data and highly summarized data, et al.

Inmon, W. H. "The Anatomy of a Data Warehouse Record." *Data Management Review* (July 1995). A description of the internal structure of a data warehouse record.

Inmon, W. H. "The Cabinet Effect." *Data base Programming/Design* (May 1991). A description of why the data warehouse-centered architecture does not degenerate into the spider web environment.

Inmon, W. H. "The Data Warehouse and Data Mining." *CACM* 39, no. 11 (November 1996). A description of the relationship between data mining and data warehouse.

Inmon, W. H. "The Data Warehouse: Managing the Infrastructure." *Data Management Review* (December 1994). A description of the data warehouse infrastructure and the budget associated with it.

Inmon, W. H. "The Data Warehouse—All Your Data at Your Fingertips." *Communications Week* (August 29, 1994). An overview of the data warehouse.

Inmon, W. H. "The Future in History." *DMR* (September 1996). A discussion of the value of historical information.

Inmon, W. H. "The Ladder of Success." *Data Management Review* (November 1995). Building and managing the data warehouse environment entails more than selecting a platform. This article outlines the many necessary steps required to achieve a successful data warehouse environment.

Inmon, W. H. "The Need for Reporting." *Data Base Programming/Design* (July 1992). The different kinds of reports found throughout the different parts of the architecture.

Inmon, W. H. "The Operational Data Store." *INFODB* 9, no. 1 (February 1995). A description of the ODS.

Inmon, W. H. "The Structure of the Data Warehouse." *Data Management Review* (August 1993). This article addresses the different levels of data found in the data warehouse.

Inmon, W. H. "Transformation Complexity." *Data Management Review* (September 1995). Why automating the transformation process is a superior idea to manually programming the transformations that are required in order to build the data warehouse.

Inmon, W. H. "Untangling the Web." *Data Base Programming Design* (May 1993). Exploring the factors that turn data into information.

Inmon, W. H. "User Reaction to the Data Warehouse." *DMR* (December 1996). A description of the different user types in data warehousing.

Inmon, W. H. "Virtual Data Warehouse: The Snake Oil of the 90's." *Data Management Review* (April 1996). A discussion of the virtual data warehouse and how the concept tries to attach itself to the legitimacy of the data warehouse.

Inmon, W. H. "Winds of Change." *Data Base Programming/Design* (January 1992). Data administration and the data warehouse—a description of how data administration evolved to where it is today.

Inmon, W. H., and Chuck Kelley. "The 12 Rules of Data Warehouse." *Data Management Review* (May 1994). A description of the defining characteristics of the data warehouse.

Inmon, W. H., and Michael Loper. "The Unified Data Architecture: A Systems Integration Solution." Auerbach Publications (1992). The original paper (republished in a revised state) suggesting that a data architecture was in order for future systems development.

Inmon, W. H., and Phyliss Koslow. "Commandeering Mainframe Database for Data Warehouse Use." *Application Development Trends* (August 1994). A discussion of optimal data warehouse use inside the mainframe.

Inmon, W. H., and Sue Osterfelt. "Data Patterns Say the Darndest Things." *Computerworld* (February 3, 1992). A description of the usage of the data warehouse in the DSS community and how informational processing can be derived from a warehouse.

Jordan, Arthur. "Data Warehouse Integrity: How Long and Bumpy the Road?" *Data Management Review* (March 1996). A discussion of the issues of data quality inside the data warehouse.

Kador, John. "One on One." Interview with Bill Inmon, Midrange Systems (October 27, 1995). A discussion about data warehouse with Bill, including some of the history of how data warehouse came to be.

Kimball, Ralph, and Kevin Strehlo. "Why Decision Support Fails and How To Fix It." *Datamation* (June 1994). A good description of fact tables and star joins, with a lengthy discussion about Ralph's approach to data warehouse and decision support.

Kimball, Ralph. "Is ER Modelling Hazardous to DSS?" *Data Warehouse Report* (Winter 1995). A dialogue on dimensional modelling versus ER modelling.

Konrad, Walecia. "Smoking Out the Elusive Smoker." *BusinessWeek* (March 16, 1992). A description of database marketing in the advertising restricted marketing environment.

Lambert, Bob. "Break Old Habits to Define Data Warehousing Requirements." *Data Management Review*. A description of how the end user should be approached to determine DSS requirements.

Lambert, Bob. "Data Warehousing Fundamentals: What You Need to Know to Succeed." *Data Management Review* (March 1996). Several significant strategies for data warehousing to guide you through a successful implementation.

Laney, Doug. "Are OLAP and OLTP Like Twins?" *DMR* (December 1996). A comparison of the two environments.

"Liberate Your Data." *Forbes* (March 7, 1994). An interesting but naive article about the data warehouse as viewed from the uninformed businessperson.

Myer, Andrea. "An Interview with Bill Inmon." *Inside Decisions* (March 1996). An interview discussing the start of data warehousing, use of data warehousing for competitive advantage, the origins of Prism Solutions, building the first data warehouse, etc.

O'Mahoney, Michael. "Revolutionary Breakthrough in Client/Server Data Warehouse Development." *Data Management Review* (July 1995). A description of older legacy development methodologies versus modern iterative methodologies.

Rudin, Ken. "Parallelism in the Database Layer." *DMR* (December 1996). An excellent discussion of the differences between DSS parallelism and OLTP parallelism.

Rudin, Ken. "Who Needs Scalable Systems." *DMR* (November 1996). A good discussion of the issues of scalability in the data warehouse environment.

Sloan, Robert, and Hal Green. "An Information Architecture for the Global Manufacturing Enterprise." Auerbach Publications (1993). A description of information architecture in the large-scale manufacturing environment.

Swift, Ron. "Creating Value Through a Scalable Data Warehouse Framework." *DMR* (November 1996). A very nice discussion of the data warehousing issues scale.

Tanler Richard. "Taking Your Data Warehouse to a New Dimension on the Intranet." *Data Management Review* (May 1996). A discussion of the different components of the data warehouse as they relate to the intranet.

Tanler, Richard. "Data Warehouses and Data Marts: Choose Your Weapon." *Data Management Review* (February 1996). A description of the differences between data marts and the current level detail of the data warehouse.

"The Doctor of DSS." DBMS Interview. *DBMS magazine* (July 1994). An interview with Ralph Kimball.

Thiessen, Mark. "Proving the Data Warehouse to Management and Customers: Where Are the Savings?" A presentation given at the 1994 Data Warehouse Conference; for foils and handouts.

Verity, John W. and Russell Mitchell. "A Trillion Byte Weapon." *BusinessWeek* (July 31, 1995). A description of some of the larger data warehouses that have been built and how they play a role in business competition.

Wahl, Dan, and Duane Hufford. "A Case Study: Implementing and Operating an Atomic Database." *Data Resource Management Journal* (April 1992). A description of the U.S. Army DSS data architecture.

Welch, J. D. "Providing Customized Decision Support Capabilities: Defining Architectures." Auerbach Publications (1990). Discusses decision support systems and architecture (based on the PacTel Cellular DSS architecture).

Winsberg, Paul. "Modeling the Data Warehouse and the Data Mart." *INFODB* (June 1996). A description of architecture and modelling as it relates to different types of data warehouses.

Wright, George. "Developing a Data Warehouse." *DMR* (October 1996). A very good discussion of snapshots and the basic structures of data warehouse.

PINE CONE SYSTEMS TECH TOPICS

1. MONITORING DATA WAREHOUSE ACTIVITY. Activity in the data warehouse needs to be monitored for a variety of reasons. This tech topic describes monitoring techniques and considerations, as well as a description of why activity monitoring needs to be done.
2. CHARGEBACK IN THE DATA WAREHOUSE DSS ENVIRONMENT. Chargeback is an extremely useful way to get the end user to take responsibility for the resources that are being consumed. This tech topic addresses the issues of chargeback.
3. ITERATIVE DEVELOPMENT USING A DATA MODEL. Data modelling is an essential part of the data warehouse design process. This tech topic explains how iterative development can be done and at the same time how the data model is incorporated into the development process.
4. WHAT IS A DATA MART? Data marts are a natural emanation from the data warehouse. This tech topic outlines the salient characteristics of the data mart.
5. DATA MINING—AN ARCHITECTURE. Using the data warehouse is an art. This tech topic relates the underlying architecture of the data warehouse to the sophisticated way in which the data warehouse can be used.
6. DATA MINING—EXPLORING THE DATA. Once the data is gathered and organized, and the architecture for exploitation has been built, the task remains to use the data. This tech topic addresses how data can be mined, once the architecture is built.
7. BUILDING THE DATA MART OR THE DATA WAREHOUSE FIRST? While the data mart is a companion to the data warehouse, data mart vendors try to encourage people to build the data mart without building the data warehouse. This tech topic addresses the issues relevant to this important design decision.
8. MONITORING DATA WAREHOUSE DATA. While activity monitoring is very important, so is monitoring the data itself in the data warehouse. The growth of the data, the quality of the data, the actual content of the data are all at stake in this issue.
9. DATA WAREHOUSE ADMINISTRATION. With DSS and data warehouse comes the need to manage the environment. A new organizational function has arisen—data warehouse administration. This tech topic addresses the charter of data warehouse administration and other important data management issues.
10. METADATA IN THE DATA WAREHOUSE: A STATEMENT OF VISION. Metadata is an important part of the data warehouse environment. Metadata has a dual, conflicting role. In some cases, metadata must be shared; in other cases, it needs to be managed

autonomously. This Tech topic addresses the distributed metadata architecture which allows metadata to simultaneously be distributed and to
be managed autonomously.

11. DATA WAREHOUSE ADMINISTRATION IN THE ORGANIZATION.
    Once the need for data warehouse administration is recognized, there is
    the question—where should the DWA function be placed in the organi-
    zation? This tech topic addresses the issues of the organization place-
    ment of the DWA function.

12. MANAGING THE REFRESHMENT PROCESS. Data periodically needs
    to be refreshed from the legacy environment into the data warehouse.
    The refreshment process is much more complex than one would ever
    imagine. This tech topic addresses the issues of data warehouse refresh-
    ment.

13. DATA STRATIFICATION IN THE DATA WAREHOUSE. How do you
    tell someone what is inside a 1 terabyte data warehouse? How many
    customers? Of what type? Of what age? Living where? Buying how
    much per year? This tech topic addresses the technique of stratifying
    data in order to create a library "table of contents" that describes what
    actual content of data there is inside a data warehouse.

Pine Cone Systems can be reached at 303-221-4000; Fax: 303-221-4010.

BOOKS

Brackett, Mike. *The Data Warehouse Challenge*. New York: John Wiley & Sons,
    Inc., Copyright 1996.
Devlin, Barry. *Data Warehouse: From Architecture to Implementation*. Reading,
    Massachusetts: Addison Wesley, Copyright 1997.
Inmon, W. H. *Building the Data Warehouse*, 2d ed. New York: John Wiley &
    Sons, Inc., Copyright 1996. (1st edition 1992)
Inmon, W. H., Imnoff, Claudia, Battas, Greg. *Building the Operational Data
    Store*. New York: John Wiley & Sons, Inc., Copyright 1996.
Inmon, W. H. *Information Systems Architecture: Development in the '90s*. New
    York: John Wiley & Sons, Inc., Copyright 1992.
Inmon, W.H., Welch, J. D., Glassey, Katherine L., *Managing the Data Warehouse*.
    New York: John Wiley & Sons, Inc., Copyright 1997.
Inmon, W. H. *Rdb/VMS: Developing the Data Warehouse*. New York: John Wiley
    & Sons, Inc., Copyright 1993.
Inmon, W. H. *Third Wave Processing: Database Machines and Decision Support
    Systems*. New York: John Wiley & Sons, Inc., Copyright 1990.
Inmon, W. H., Hackathorn, R.D. *Using the Data Warehouse*. New York: John
    Wiley & Sons, Inc., Copyright 1994.

Inmon, W. H., John A. Zachman, and Jonathan G. Geiger. *Data Stores, Data Warehousing and the Zachman Framework*. New York: McGraw-Hill, 1997.

Kelly, Sean. *Data Warehousing—The Key to Mass Customization*. New York: John Wiley & Sons, Inc., Copyright 1994.

Kimball, Ralph. *The Data Warehouse Toolkit*. New York: John Wiley Sons, Inc., Copyright 1996.

Love, Bruce. *Enterprise Information Technologies*. New York: John Wiley & Sons, Inc., Copyright 1993.

Parsaye, Kamran, and Marc Chignell. *Intelligent Database Tools and Applications*. New York: John Wiley & Sons, Inc., Copyright 1989.

BOOK REVIEWS

Information Systems Management (Winter 1997) Bookisms. Paul Gray, "Mining for Data Warehouse Gems." A review of several books on data warehousing.

Index

265